TESTIMONIALS

"Toss in your stilettos for steel caps ladies!

This is a book that will inspire you to find your own feet and do what you want instead of what you think you should be doing. It's a book that will inspire you and dispel any self-doubt but more importantly, motivate normal, everyday women of all ages and from all walks of life to take control of their financial futures.

This is not a book on the Wars of the Roses but about finding what truly floats your boat and ultimately makes you happy. After all, isn't that what life is all about?"

Cherie Barber,
Australia's Top Renovator & TV Personality

"Lynette Gray's book is aptly named 'Women in Workboots' as the author walks her talk having worked all her life in a male dominated industry. She is a leading expert and a great mentor for women, teaching them that they can do any job that they choose to do.

This book is a must read for women seeking inspiration and the courage to go for it and take up any role in their chosen industry; to not be threatened and held back from stepping out of the so-called 'norm' for women's employment roles. It will give the reader confidence, assurance and the belief that they can indeed do anything they want.

This book will grip the reader and hold them enthralled with the thought provoking and powerfully true stories of prominent and highly successful women and gives a great insight into how women, against all odds, can achieve anything they want - there are no barriers other than those that exist in our own minds. Opportunities are out there and available to women and there are no limits to what we can do.

I highly recommend 'Women in Workboots.' It will change your thinking and your life!"

Karen Scott
International Author of 'Rising from The Rubble' and Speaker

"The glass ceiling stands defiant and resolute across much of Workplace Australia, confronting many women who dare to achieve and all too often this unseen and unacknowledged barrier to progress is not even cracked.

In Women in Workboots, Lynette Gray brilliantly captures the fears, failures and fame of women who stood tall and successfully challenged the status quo. This sometimes confronting exposé needs to be read by every company director, CEO, HR director and client.

Buy a copy today, read it and add your voice to the cause of fostering a meritocracy throughout our workforce.

Even better, buy a second copy and give it to a woman who needs encouragement to reach her destiny or someone who should be giving encouragement to women."

Neil Findlay
Queensland Logistics Council
2015: We Can Do This Thing!
Let it be your best year ever, professionally and personally.

"This book is total inspiration. Just reading the table of contents makes you realise what value lies inside. This book is not only a good read but gives an insight into what led these impressive women to achieve what they did. The lessons, tips and guidance are there to inspire another generation of 'Women in Workboots.'

The author herself has walked the talk and achieved recognition and awards for following her vision and passion. This is a book that had to be written and Lynette Gray was the one to write it."

Stephen Parr
Author of 'Take Charge of Your Money Now'

"It was satisfying to watch Lynette develop from the time she first joined Simon National Carriers and then ultimately to the point of establishing her own specialised transport business. Her initiative now, to inspire other women in the transport and other industries through the sharing of the experiences of many successful women in what are generally perceived to be male dominated industries, will prove to be a useful reminder to many of what can be achieved by "having a go."

In my roles on industry boards and in my dealings with many customers and governments, I have certainly found that the women who have chosen to "have a go" have, as well as being successful in their businesses or government roles, also on many occasions, put forward useful and different views that had not been perceived by others.

I hope this book inspires everybody who reads it to aspire to achieve whatever goals they set themselves and to become leaders in their chosen fields."

David Simon
Director
Simon National Carriers

WOMEN in WORKBOOTS

GLOBAL
PUBLISHING
G R O U P

Global Publishing Group
Australia • New Zealand • Singapore • America • London

WOMEN *in* WORKBOOTS

Inspirational Stories of

Women Who Have Broken Through the Barriers in Male Dominated Industries

LYNETTE GRAY

First Edition 2015

National Library of Australia
Cataloguing-in-Publication entry:

Creator: Gray, Lynette, 1968- author.

Women in workboots : inspirational stories of women who have
broken through the barriers in male dominated industries / Lynette Gray.

1st ed.
ISBN: 9781922118660 (paperback)

Businesswomen--Attitudes.
Businesswomen--Australia--Anecdotes.
Success in business.

650.1082

Published by Global Publishing Group
PO Box 517 Mt Evelyn, Victoria 3796 Australia
Email Info@GlobalPublishingGroup.com.au

For further information about orders:
Phone: +61 3 9739 4686 or Fax +61 3 8648 6871

This book is dedicated to all those inspirational women who know they can achieve anything they wish and have the courage to stand up for what they believe.

Lynette Gray

ACKNOWLEDGEMENTS

It has been an honour and a privilege to write this book. As with any major project, there are a number of incredible people who contributed to making this book happen and I am so grateful to them all.

Firstly, I would like to thank Darren Stephens who planted the seed that I could write this book in my mind a number of years ago and offered me regular encouragement, support and guidance in seeing it come to fruition. Thank you for believing in me and giving me one of the most exciting opportunities that will make the greatest and most valuable change to my life.

The assistance and collaboration provided by Serena Giudice, Nicole Henness, Natalie Morgan, Kathy Ross, Eleni Mitakos, Mary Koutalis, Marilyn Wood, Sharon Jurd, Heather Jones, Julie Shuttleworth, Helen Yost and Naomi Williams who were critical in helping develop the content and structure for the book as well as providing regular inspiration and invaluable contributions.

A number of other individuals allowed me to call upon them regularly for advice and information including Sharon Jurd and Helen Busse, Fletcher Searle, Basil Nuredini and Robert Hills.

Also a special thank you goes to David Simon, Neil Findlay, Stephen Parr, Karen Scott and Cherie Barber for taking the time to write a testimony and their belief in what women can achieve.

To my special friends Robyn Roger, Karen Thompson, Stephanie Clarke and Anne Duncan for your support and encouragement during my times of doubt and procrastination and the willingness to give your time and advice over the years, this has meant the world to me and I appreciate all that you have done for me.

I wish to thank my husband Trevor, who has the patience and faith in me to let me see this project through. Our boys Daniel, Timothy and Christopher for their amazing love and support of my efforts and who are all very capable and can achieve anything they want to. I would also like to acknowledge my parents, David and Noela Staib and Glen and Lorna Gray, my family Paul and Mitzi, John and Tammy, Rodney and Bernedette and all my nephews and nieces that make up our close-knit family unit.

I also acknowledge my Aunty Lorna for leading by example in whatever adversity life throws at you; never lose sight of your sense of humour.

CONTENTS

BONUS OFFER FREE

BONUS CHAPTERS
With Additional Interviews

For your free download, go to...
www.WomenInWorkboots.com.au

INTRODUCTION

I wrote this book because when I attended an International Woman's Day Queensland Transport Association Breakfast and the low percentage of women working in the transport industry became apparent to me. To my horror, it declined from 23% the previous year to 22% in that year and the numbers included the administrative women.

The speaker of the day was talking about how important it is to become a mentor to other women who want to be part of this industry. While I was sitting in that meeting I had an overwhelming urge… "I must write this book." That was the moment of conception for this project.

This is my way of giving back to an industry that has been good to me my whole life. As a small child I would sit up in the cab like "Jacky" with my father, taking the grain an hour and a half down the road to the grain silos on Queensland's Darling Downs during the harvest season. I worked at a variety of businesses including Simon National Carriers and my family's road train business prior to starting our own business. Since trucks had been a part of my life one way or another, it was a natural progression that my husband Trevor and I would eventually end up in this industry, albeit "Tonka Trucks."

> *"There are only 2 ways to do things,*
> *right and again."*
>
> *Lynette Gray*

When I was pregnant with our third son we started a refrigerated courier business that services South East Queensland. He is now a young adult. This business was conceived from a comment that a client made in passing in 1997. We basically went to the coast, bought a refrigerated truck and came home. I made up some flyers and took them around to businesses that we had an association with through our private lives or past places of work.

On the first day of business we drove down to Brisbane and we were three quarters of the way back to Toowoomba when we got our first call, with not one box in the truck. We actually turned around, drove back to Brisbane, picked up this one parcel, brought it to Toowoomba and delivered it.

"If you are passionate about what you're doing and you believe in it and you are offering a really great product at a fair price, then people are going to want to deal with you and you're on your road to success."

Serena Giudice
National Young Builder of the Year, 2014

We were in business!!!

INTRODUCTION

It is my passion to inspire, encourage and educate women in male dominated industries. I want to teach them to fish, I don't want to hand them a fish. I want to be able to just encourage people by saying, "Yes, you can do it, you can do anything" and then be there to celebrate in their successes.

It doesn't matter what it is, just enjoy what you do and don't take yourself too seriously.

Have a bit of fun along the way.

Now you have an understanding of who I am and why I've done this. In the following pages you'll find other amazing women from different types of industries who I've interviewed and who have valuable tips and resources that they can share. They can help you on your journey as well. These are their stories, straight from their own lips.

My tips for women to be more successful

1. Do what you enjoy.
    Do it with your full heart, get in there and do it.
    Don't think, just do it!
    Have fun while you're doing it.
    Laugh, have your cups of coffee and enjoy your work.

2. One of the most important things is to be rock solid; build a rock solid reputation.
    A good reputation is unquestionably one of the most tangible, marketable things you've got.
    You can't buy a good reputation so you need to honour it. You need to build trust with people.

3. One of the other important things is to take time off.
   Pick up your family and go away.
   Have time with just your family.
   Also take time off just for yourself.
   People find that in different ways. Some people think they want to go for a massage or go for a coffee or whatever.
   For me, it's sitting under a tree.

> *"Start Where you Are*
> *Use What you Have*
> *Do What you Can"*
>
> **Bob Proctor**

CHAPTER 1

Serena Giudice

National Young Builder of the Year, 2014

CHAPTER 1

Serena Giudice
Ric New Medal of Excellence – September 2009
National Young Builder of the Year, 2014
40 under 40 Award – February 2015

Serena Giudice is a Registered Builder and is the General Manager of Kevin Giudice & Co / Geraldton Homes since the death of her father in 2009. Serena received the Ric New Medal of Excellence in September 2009 and was named National Young Builder of the Year by the Master Builders Association in 2014. Most recently she has been awarded the 40 under 40 Award by WA Business News which celebrates Western Australia's 40 leading business entrepreneurs under the age of 40.

Since January 2008 Serena has been Master Builders Association Geraldton Branch Committee Member and held the office of Branch Chairman since January 2012. She also is involved with the Construction Apprenticeship Mentoring Scheme (CAMS) which is a major new initiative of the Master Builders Australia to improve apprenticeship completions and also enhances career opportunities in the building and construction industry.

I hope winning National Young Builder of the Year will act as an inspiration for other woman in the construction industry. You don't necessarily need a trade background to run your own company. We need more women to choose the construction industry as a career path. When Michaelia Cash presented my award she said 89% of the construction workforce is male, compared to 54% for all industries.

The statistics are disturbing but a lot of people particularly women don't understand how fantastic the building industry is and how much opportunity there is out there. I would have loved to had a career adviser at a high school talk about career paths in the building and construction industry, it wasn't even suggested to me and I think that's really sad. Being from a family of builders, you would have thought that construction was on my radar but it wasn't. I didn't even consider it.

How long after you left school did you start to think, okay, I might go and join Dad and become a builder or was it just on weekends that you started to do more and more and it sort of grew from there or what actually happened? How did that come about?

It's really hard for kids at high school to know what they want to do for the rest of their lives and I was certainly one of those people who had no idea. I kind of just went to university because that was the next step. I studied environmental science for 12 months and hated it. I was away from home for the first time and went from country living with my mum and dad to living in Perth by myself.

It was definitely a bit of a culture shock. Anyway, I didn't particularly enjoy it so I ended up coming back home. After that I dabbled in another career (computer systems engineering). Again I did that for 12 months but didn't really enjoy it and couldn't find my passion.

Dad saw that I wasn't happy and I was working part-time at a local firm and the work was really repetitive, which is to be expected when you first start out in a career, I suppose. But when you're installing the same software program on 100 computers in a row because you've got a contract for a school, it definitely isn't the most exciting thing. It's not that I didn't appreciate the opportunity that was given to me but it just wasn't for me and Dad saw that I wasn't happy so he said, "Look, why don't you come out here and give this a go and try something different for 12 months? We're quite busy. We need the extra help." A few weeks later I found myself at my Dad's office. My first lesson was how to use the photocopier.

I really enjoyed maths and the sciences at school so joining Dad and his business, learning how to schedule labour and materials. Prepare quotations, working with our subcontractors was fantastic. In hindsight, I was forced to deal with people all the time and at that age when I wasn't very confident. It definitely brought me out of my shell. That's how I first went into the building industry, I just kind of fell into it.

The award you've got is just incredible. Can you tell us about it?

It's National Young Builder of the Year for 2014. The awards were held in Canberra. I was nominated by the Western Australian branch of the Master Builders Association to represent our state. It was beyond exciting to be chosen as the best in Australia, I've never seen my Mum or my family so proud. There wasn't a dry eye in the house. I am the first woman to ever win a national construction award with the Master Builders. There are so many talented ladies out there, I was the first, but certainly won't be the last!

Tell me about your first experience with building as a kid.

Dad used to take us out to the building sites. Back then, before chemical curing was readily available we had to "pond the slabs". This involved placing a dam of shallow water on top of a newly poured slab to stop it drying out/curing too quickly. Towards the end of the day, we'd go to site to refill the pools of water and to make sure the little dams were intact. That's probably my earliest memory; of going to a building site and helping Dad. Although, we may have spent more time throwing boondies (balls of yellow fill sand) at each other than helping Dad! I'm one of four so we used to have great fun. It a Western Australian twist on the traditional snowball fight.

What's been the satisfying moment in your career thus far?

Winning the award, by far. That was a huge thing, to be named the best in the whole of Australia. It was just mind blowing. It was a real confidence boost after losing my dad in 2009. I had been running the company without him since then (with the help of my loyal team). Dad did prepare me for it though. He stepped down from working full time when he decided to run for a state government position in 2006. This allowed me to gain more managerial experience while knowing he was only a phone call away.

Dad always said to us, when we were kids that he did not care what we chose to do in life, as long as we tried our hardest and we tried to be the best at it. I suppose this award was a huge validation of that. I'd like to think he'd be really proud and that he was looking down at what we've done with the company and kind of say, "That's my girl."

How have your motivations changed, especially since 2009?

2009 was really tricky. I had the stress of losing Dad, Geraldton is a progressive city, but it is definitely a small city. When Dad passed away there were a lot of rumours going around. People were talking because Dad passed away. Some people assumed the company was going to close and that caused a loss consumer confidence.

We overcame that by continuing to build beautiful homes, with the attention to detail that we're proud of, all while offering brilliant customer service to our wonderful clients. We continued to win awards (the Building Excellence Awards in the Midwest region) and before we knew it all those rumours just disappeared. Building with excellence, having really happy customers, positive reviews while maintaining relationships with our amazing subcontractors.

If you had the chance to start over again, what would you do differently?

I would probably not stuff around with other career options. I would have gone straight to the building industry to start with and not wasted those two years.

What advice would you give college students who want to be a builder or a carpenter because I understand that the two are completely different?

Make sure you are organised. Work to develop good relationships with people. Start small and build your knowledge and experience over time. There are several different paths on the road to running a building company. You can get an apprenticeship, work as a carpenter, bricklayer, plumber etc. You can study at university to get a degree in Construction management. You can work in a building company as a supervisor, estimator scheduler and apply for your registration after proving your experience. You don't need to be experienced in hands on work. Although that can definitely help you be a success.

Personally I worked my way up within the organisation, building my knowledge over a period of time. I took on more and more responsibility with supervision and construction scheduling and developed skills in construction / project management. After 10 years I applied for my builders registration. That involved sitting three exams, then proving my experience and that I was financially ok. Getting my builders registration was a notable highlight of my career.

What are your true ideals?

One is being the best and being excellent in whatever I choose to do and that's one of the reasons we chose the motto for our company, which is, *"Building with Excellence."*

Integrity and honesty is really important to me. Sometimes when people deal with builders it's really hard for them to know exactly what they're getting. Part of my role is educating my potential clients so that they have a good idea of what to expect and what is and is not included in the price.

Some of the pricing out there can be quite deceptive. For example, you'll open up the paper and there is an advert in there that says you'll get this house for this amount of money but at the end of the day, you're going to have to spend an extra $60,000 to finish it off because there's no painting included and they haven't taken into account any site works. There are all those hidden costs that aren't factored into the bargain prices. I like to be honest and up front with clients, I want them to be happy when we've finished our work. There's nothing better than handing over a home that is finished beautifully to really happy clients, it's a hug motivator for me.

What have some of your challenges been and what have you learnt from them?

The biggest challenge would have been losing my dad and dealing with that grief while knowing that there was a business to run. That the company and all the people that worked there depended on me. That was always that at the back of my mind when I first started back. My wonderful team at Geraldton Homes were a huge help. Without their support it would have been an impossible challenge.

Would it be fair to say that would be one of your greatest fears, letting someone down?

Yes, I don't like to let people down. I like to set realistic expectations. I like to make sure that I've got work for my trade and I like to make sure that my clients are really happy with our finished product. Letting people down is my greatest fear.

What would you consider to be your greatest achievement? Can you pinpoint why you were chosen for that award, Young Builder of the Year? Was it because you were successful as a woman or do you think there were other factors in winning that award?

No, there were definitely other factors. The criteria was to be

- Under 40 (being referred to as young is my favourite part of the award)

- Be a registered builder

- To have at least two years in business

- To maintain quality of workmanship and high safety standards

- Demonstrate sound business management and ethical conduct

- Be a financially sound business

- Demonstrate a high level of client satisfaction and customer service

- Be held in high regard by the industry peers

- Be actively involved in the Master Builders

- Contribute to the betterment of the industry

I had to send an application that dealt with each of those points. I think one of the biggest positives is that I'm actively involved in the Master Builders Association. I've been chairman. This is my fourth year as chairman of Midwest and the Northwest of the Master Builders of Western Australia.

I have also been involved in a mentoring program to teach or encourage apprentices to finish their apprenticeships. There is a problem with apprentices dropping out in their first and second years. We aim to offer them the support they needed to encourage them to stay in the industry.

To be held in high regard by the industry peers is my favourite criteria. I rang up a couple of builders that work in the same areas as I do and they were more than happy to give me amazing references. To know that your competitors are saying really positive and lovely things about you, was an amazing part of the journey.

Another favourite one is, whenever I finish a house I give my customers a client satisfaction form and they fill it out, so I sent five or six of those through and they had glowing reviews from people who were really happy after dealing with us.

On the night of the national construction awards, I was approached by some of the judges on the panel. I had never met them before and didn't know who they were. They were lovely and made a point of saying, "I just want you to know that you didn't win this because you are a woman. You won it on your own merit and because you're an outstanding candidate." That was a highlight of the night.

I received a lot of media attention about this award, probably because I'm a woman and there aren't a lot of women in the construction industry. In my own mind, gender is irrelevant and everyone should be judged on their merits, not their gender. So I had mixed feelings about it. On the other hand, it was a great opportunity to get the word out there, to try and inspire other women to consider a career path in the building industry.

How has being a builder affected your family and your personal life?

It has affected it at all. I'm actually still single and I'd love to have a family. I just haven't met the right person yet. Hopefully he'll come along soon.

What does a day in the life of Serena Giudice consist of?

It's funny. You go to sleep and you dream about work. You jump in the shower in the morning and you think about what you're going to get up to that day. I have a morning meeting with my construction supervisor who looks after all my sites for me. We talk about what we're going to do or what we're going to achieve for that day.

If there's any problem throughout the day, he'll give me call and I'll go to the site and have a look at it and we'll resolve whatever issues need to be resolved. If there are no issues and I don't get a phone call, things just continue as usual.

There's operational and managerial work. A lot of my day consists of talking to clients, subcontractors and suppliers. There is a huge complicated chain of work that goes into building a new home. Coordinating everything to happen at the right time is a challenge.

Maintaining good relationships with people is really important. If you're pleasant to deal with, you pay your bills on time, you're a fair person that treats people with respect, people will enjoy dealing with you. Every day is always different. At the moment, we're looking at putting together a marketing campaign, to try and get our business name out there a little bit more. We find it hard to compete with big project builders advertising budgets. In the past we rarely advertised, but there seems to be a lot of new people in town, we want to try and get our message out to them, to let them know that we are here and we are a great builder that is a pleasure to deal with.

What would be the strangest thing you've ever done?

Buying a horse was a bit weird, I suppose, at this age. I used to ride as a kid and I hadn't ridden properly for about 15 years. I started riding a friend's horse and I enjoyed it so much that I decided to get my own.

It's a great way to wind down. It's physical exercise and it's hard work looking after them but it's the best thing I've ever done. I just really enjoy it … but maybe that's not strange.

It is a great way to de-stress. You're just out there, you and your horse and you're riding on the river and it's just beautiful. It's a great way to just let everything go.

Another strange thing that happened when I went travelling to Europe with my brother and sister in 2004. We went to this crypt in Rome and it was decorated with the bones of all these people that had died of the plague hundreds of years ago.

They buried the dead outside of the city and after a period of time, the monks went out and dug them all up. It was impossible to know who each bone belonged to, so they decorated a shrine with them. There is nothing so eerie than seeing human bones arranged in patterns on the wall, there were images of roses created with bones from a spinal column. It was one of the most amazing, breathtaking, mind blowing and saddest thing I've ever seen. Every wall and ceiling was covered with human remains.

So there we are, overwhelmed by this amazing experience, standing outside the crypt, when we spot Mel Gibson. The mood quickly turned, we morphed into giggling school girls, struck by the power of celebrity! That was weird.

What would you say are the five key elements to starting and running a successful business?

Integrity, honesty, good relationships, have a clear purpose, making sure your staff is aware of that and never lose sight of it. It also really helps to get a bit of independent advice. Running a small business means that you have to be a jack of all trades, it's not like a big company where everyone has their specific roles.

Do you believe there's some sort of pattern or formula to becoming successful at what you do?

I think it's really important to have passion and belief in what you do. If you are offering a really good product at a fair price, then people are going to want to deal with you and you're on the road to success. You need to be driven and self-motivated. A great well thought out business plan doesn't hurt either.

Looking back, is there one thing that you wish you'd understood about the construction industry before you ever started your career?

It's more about building relationships than building houses in a way. One, you want to do a good job. You want to be excellent at that and everything else flows from there but the relationships that you build are so important. You build relationships with your clients, you build relationships with your suppliers, your subcontractors and I have said this before, but women are really good at building relationships. They're really good at communicating and developing loyalty, respect and trust in those relationships.

What is your favourite book?

I love reading and there are so many great novels to choose from. 'One Flew over the Cuckoo's Nest' was a great read, the power struggle between Nurse Ratched and Mcmurphy was fascinating. 'To Kill a Mockingbird' is a beautiful book. 'Pride and Prejudice' appealed to the romantic in me and like many others I love the 'Game of Thrones' series.

'The Alchemist', was a book full of little gems of wisdom
When I was a child I loved the Narnia series, I've re-read those books so many times I've lost count.

Finally, what do you want to do when you grow up?

I'd love to find the right person and start a family, I look forward to the challenge of running a successful business and growing a family.

My aunt is a huge inspiration for me. She worked full time raised her family, had the children at work. It seemed to work really well for them, so I'm sure it will work for me too.

There are parallels with us as well, Lynette, because Dad ran the business from home for a number of years before he actually moved to a dedicated office, so his work was a part of day to day life. Our workers were always around. We had the two-way in the kitchen.

I don't think it's a bad thing for kids to see their parents working from home. A good work ethic is something really important to impart to your children.

Is there something specific that you would like to tell the readers?

I think that gender is absolutely irrelevant. Work hard, do a really good job and people will notice you for that. They'll respect you for everything else will fall into place. It's often a struggle in the beginning but it's a struggle for anyone starting a new business. Persevere at it and you try your hardest, try and be the best person you can be, start small, aim for the stars.

Do the right thing by people and don't burn bridges you just never know what's around the corner. Don't take things too personally. I think I just spat out a whole lot of clichés, but then they're clichés for a reason, there's wisdom and truth there.

CHAPTER 2

Nicole Henness

Senior Firefighter with Fire & Rescue NSW

CHAPTER 2

Nicole Henness
Senior Firefighter with Fire & Rescue NSW

Nicole Henness was teaching Physical Education, a subject that she loved, as she considers it's the most important subject in high school; teaching kids how to live a healthy lifestyle. But when you're getting the students that think it is a bludge subject and not taking it seriously it makes you feel a little bit dejected. She started to look at other occupations and became a firefighter with Fire and Rescue NSW in 2002 and this career has given her many satisfying moments.

How did you become involved with the NSW Fire Authority?

I had a bit of a mid-life crisis and wasn't enjoying my job as a high school teacher. I knew a lot of firefighters who all loved their job and it's an active job and I like to be active. I was also desperate for a change.

I trained as a P.E. teacher because I like to help people and contribute to society in some way. Applying for the NSW Fire Brigade, as it was known then, made sense to me as it ticked all of my boxes for a career change.

Unfortunately I struck out the first year I applied. The second year I tried out I was accepted.

"If you don't like the road you're walking, start paving another one."

What sparked your interest in being a firefighter?

Every day is different. You don't know what you're going to get, you don't know how busy it's going to be or where you're going to go, who you're going to meet.

It's a physical job and being active a lot of the time helps to keep up an active lifestyle. Due to the nature of the job we are expected to keep fit. It would be a difficult and tiring occupation if you weren't fit.

I just like to be hands-on with things. I'm not someone who likes to sit indoors or sit at a computer or be stagnant for too long. It makes me feel suffocated. I like to keep learning things to be active and also being able to assist and educate people. People don't want to do a lot of the things that we're doing but I don't mind getting dirty and sweaty. This job provides me with all those qualities that I desire.

I don't have to put makeup on to go to work like a lot of other women who might work in offices. I would feel pressured to do so if I worked in a corporate type job. You know, with this job you put your uniform on and you're ready and out you go.

What advice would you give someone wanting to embark on the career of a firefighter?

A lot of applicants don't realise how much night shift we work and that we work a lot of weekends. People who wish to apply, need to do a bit of homework beforehand; so there are no surprises for them if they get in.

You need to be able to work as a team and respect rank because there is a structure to our service. You need to be able to work within a team, accept your part of the job in that team, be willing to learn and keep your eyes and ears open. Awareness and communication is paramount for safety.

You need to be physically and mentally/emotionally fit. Strength and aerobic training prior to the PAT (physical aptitude test) is necessary especially if you have been quite sedentary.

Everyone has different experiences from previous occupations and also from this one, but we all have the same core training. As you go along you pick up different things/techniques from different people so I think it's important to always be open to that sort of thing; be able to work with a variety of different people in different situations.

You would have seen some failures and successes in your time as a firefighter. What have you learned from them?

People do perceive things differently and will respond to the same situation differently. Sometimes there's not a right or a wrong, it's just someone's perception of what can be effective and sometimes things might not go as well as planned. The whole idea is to learn from those experiences. In reference to the actual job, if something could have been done better, or things didn't go as planned, if it's a multi-agency job or victims were involved, if something unexpected occurred, we have a debrief. We can debrief with other stations or we debrief amongst ourselves and we say, "Okay, how did that go?", or How is everyone feeling?" etc.

Sometimes everything we did worked well and that's really good or we look at other options that may have also been useful. If something works well that's great as that's the result you want. I think it's important to praise others and each other when a job is performed well. I know it's nice to hear my boss say to someone that I/his crew did really well at an incident.

At other times we stumble across things along the way that prevent us from doing the job as effectively. It may be nothing to do with us, it may be to do with the environment or safety issues that come with our job but then we look at that and we say, "Hey, what have we learned from this particular situation?"

So, what I have learnt is that life isn't perfect, as even when we work through something the way we've been taught, we often have to deal with hiccups along the way. That is simply the nature of our job. I have learnt that praise and constructive feedback is appreciated, and that to share knowledge and ask questions is important.

> *"You are braver than you believe, stronger than you seem and smarter than you think."*
>
> *A.A. Milne*

What is your greatest fear and how do you manage that fear on site?

In this job, anyone's personal fear would be getting caught in a fire that's hard to get out of. The thing with our brigade is that we don't put ourselves in danger. It is a dangerous job, you know, but we're not going to put ourselves in danger. We assess the situation and we hopefully prevent injury from happening.

I know that if I'm not comfortable with doing something then I'm not going to put myself or my coworkers at risk and my boss would not do that. It's all about getting the job done without getting people injured. We are all safety officers on the ground. Everyone keeps an eye out for things and we communicate with each other to let everyone know those different aspects that are dangerous or could become dangerous. That aspect of team work as well as following operating guidelines gets the job done without anyone getting hurt.

In a situation where you're fighting some fire all around you and you're communicating with other fighters on the ground, is that through voice? How do you communicate?

We have radios. These radios are mobile, hand-held radios that can fit in our suits. We do have a few hand signals for when we are in the line of sight.

You can train all you like in an ideal situation but in reality when you go out, the scene is always dramatically different from your training. Just knowing what to say and how to say it with as few words as possible... Aim to get the message across succinctly.

How has this change in career, from a high school teacher to a firefighter, affected your family life?

My partner works for the aviation fire service, (Aviation Rescue and Firefighting), so we both know what our jobs entail but his is different from mine. We understand each other like the shift work but sometimes you come home and you're grumpy because you've been really busy all night or whatever.

The major thing is that the shift work makes me feel like I'm running on a 75% full tank of fuel and that tank never gets filled. I think we get used to it and we learn to deal with it.

I'm definitely happy now in the job I'm doing. I found teaching a very draining and exhausting job in a different way that was harder for me. It's emotionally draining dealing with young people and it can be tiring trying to always do and say the appropriate thing.

I loved the subject I was teaching but because it was PDHPE, students thought it was a bit of a bludge subject, whereas I think it's really important. It becomes disheartening after a while, trying to impart knowledge and share your enthusiasm when many of the kids don't seem interested. I think my expectations were too high to teach.

What are your five key elements for being successful as a firefighter? What are three pieces of advice?

You need to be able to get on well with people and work well in a team. We work closely with one another in the station. We're basically always together with day shift and night shift. We travel everywhere together. It's about accommodating different personality types and working with them towards a common goal…. That comes with age and experience.

Communication. Being able to communicate and to accept differences of opinion and work towards the most effective ways to achieve results. To a certain extent, it's about being open and honest and being yourself because I don't think you can be happy in a job where you're not.

Learning to accept and work with people from all walks of life, with different mental and physical strengths, from a variety of cultural backgrounds.

Obviously females haven't been in the job as long because they were not considered as physically strong as men. However, we need many types of people from diverse backgrounds and FRNSW recognises this fact and so is an equal opportunity employer.

"Do one thing every day that scares you."

Eleanor Roosevelt

Keeping fit is necessary. Knowing that certain people on the crew are going to be better suited for doing certain things due to previous training, or size/height etc.

For instance, because I'm of a lighter build, when we'd have to gain entry into places I would generally be the one going through the window.

There are some women on the job who are going to be bigger and stronger than some of the guys so knowing your crew well enough to know who is best suited for each role is handy. We're expected to be able to do everything, but then it's that team work and common sense that allows efficiency on the job; whether that be at a fire, a rescue, a motor vehicle accident, assisting ambulance or police, rescuing animals or dealing with hazardous materials...everything involves efficient team work.

What would have been your most satisfying moment? Do you have a particular job where you were relieved by or satisfied with the outcome?

There are lots of jobs that we finish and we say, "You know, that was a good job." One recent job that sticks in my mind; when I knew I used an effective technique on the hose line to knock down the fire quickly, and my boss recognised this.

Generally, my career offers many satisfying moments, but it's nice to think I have done well and then have that reinforced by others, with their appraisal of my actions.

If you could offer a first-time female looking to get involved in the firefighting industry, what piece of advice would it be?

Not to give up because it's not a job that you necessarily just apply and can get into easily. FRNSW only recruit once a year.

If it's something you really want to do, keep trying because it is a good job and it's one of those jobs people do stay in for a long time because they do enjoy it. It has its pros and cons but if you can handle shiftwork the pros outweigh the cons. For a female, getting into the job if you have come from a job that doesn't involve physical work, you would need to train to get up to speed.

You need to know about the job you're applying for and make sure you want to do all aspects of that role. I spoke to people before I got into the job and I went to my local station and the station commander said, "Well, the door is always open, come in for a chat. He would say, "You know you're going to break nails and you're going to get dirty."

Hahahaha… I think I may have had a dress on when I dropped by that day! But so what. That's a given. There are plenty of people who don't realise how dirty and sweaty you can get doing this job and that's often without even going into a fire!

Describe a typical day in your life from when you get up on a normal day, whatever normal might be for you.

It's a very early start. We do domestic chores at our station. The pump driver who checks the pump, the inventory and we check and run the equipment to make sure that it's operating properly.

We check local hydrants. We have to make sure that they're accessible, operating and that they're indicated correctly on the telegraph poles.

If they're not and we cannot find water quickly, a fire can escalate in no time. We sometimes do a brigade exercise, or what we call a pre-incident plan. We basically go to a business or factory site and find out information that is relevant to us if a fire occurred there. For instance, what hazards are on site, what sort of fire protection they have, where the sprinkler/booster pumps are, how many people are present at different times of the day, exits etc.

Occasionally we are required to educate preschool and primary aged kids. There is also a road rescue education programme especially designed for high school students.

A couple of pre-schoolers might be a bit overwhelmed but generally they're really excited. They'll go on remembering these basic fire safety behaviours. If we can teach kids, they go home and sometimes they're better informed than their parents. Some young kids even knew not to put water on an oil fire or kitchen fire. I have in the past also taken part in fire safety education for seniors. We might not do all these things every shift but these are examples of the sort of work we do.

Most of our stations have gyms because we are expected to keep fit. We also do some sort of drill on equipment or SOG's to keep up to scratch with everything, even when we are not at an incident. Then, of course, amongst all of this, we are attending our fire calls.

Sometimes you might get a fire call and you may get another one straight after that, so you might be out for a few hours. You may not get to eat when you want to eat, or do your study etc...

You never know what's going to happen and that's the joy of the job.

If you're moving up the ranks there is compulsory study to do, so you are expected to keep up with that too.

If you could talk to one person from history, who would it be and why?

This may sound like a paradox but my passion is dancing. I would have loved to have met and danced with Gene Kelly. When I was growing up he had a big influence on my dancing. I used to watch a lot of old Hollywood/golden- age era movies and that's how my love of dance and performance grew.

Gene Kelly did everything. He acted, choreographed, directed, did all his own stunts, and did it all with style and class. That inspiration resulted in my performing and competing in '40s and '50s style dancing with a partner - rock'n'roll, swing, jitterbug - but I have roots in jazz, tap and contemporary.

I've also been successful in cabaret styles like fan dancing and comedic routines and I had a troupe that went to New York to perform. We also did corporate and club gigs and birthday parties, and were part of productions that went to different cities.

What do you want to do when you grow up?

I think this is my 'grown up' job. I've had a variety of fun jobs that involved travel so I see my current occupation as my adult job. I think I've been pretty fortunate with what I've done so far.

Where do you see yourself in the next 10 or 20 years?

Hopefully in 20 years I'll almost be retired. I see myself in the job but maybe in 15 years not as a frontline firefighter, maybe in a different role. I'd like to spread my wings in the meantime and learn different roles/ aspects of the FRNSW to keep motivated and growing.

"Don't let what you find is hard to control your mind.
Set yourself free.
Confront what you fear head on and turn those
struggles into the building blocks of your future."

Lynette Gray

CHAPTER 3

Natalie Morgan

Darren Morgan Racing
Australian Top Fuel Champions
2011, 2012, 2013, 2014

CHAPTER 3

Natalie Morgan
Darren Morgan Racing

Australian Top Fuel Champions
2011, 2012, 2013, 2014

Natalie Morgan is the Business Manager for Darren Morgan Racing which includes financial management of the business as well as coordination of the logistics, corporate entertainment, marketing, merchandise and catering for the Darren Morgan Racing team. She has been involved in the motorsport industry for the last 9 years and together with her husband, Darren, run one of Australia's most successful motorsport teams, Darren Morgan Racing (DMR), which was established in 2007. DMR is an innovative racing team in marketing programs for their partners and outperform other teams consistently. Their key values of teamwork, commitment, passion and win at all costs attitude has been instrumental in their record winning performance.

My husband Darren had actually been involved in motorsport all of his adult life. He built and drove various types of drag racing vehicles before crewing in Top Fuel for Cowin Family Racing in Australia and USA from 1996 to 2004. In 2004 Darren was requested to put a team together for a local motorsport family, Rocky Lamattina & Sons. Darren put the package together – purchased the vehicle and spare parts from the USA, trained the crew, and organised the construction of the specially designed race semi-trailer which is a mobile workshop. Darren won his first Australian Top Fuel Championship in his rookie year of driving Top

Fuel in 2004/05 for the Lamattina's which also included breaking track records and holding the Australian Record for Elapsed Time of 4.666 seconds over the quarter mile. In 2006 the Lamattina family decided they would like to drive themselves, so they took over the driving duties from Darren. We were left in the position where Darren had won the Australian Championship and was at the top of his sport but had no team to drive for. Encouraged by local community members, we formed our own team and company to run the new team.

In order to form your team, how did you get backing and create that sense of community?

Our business was formed with some partners, one of whom was Darren's cousin, Colin Beasley, who was a very successful farmer in our district. He was a very entrepreneurial man and was really focused and was also a speedway man and into motorsports. He was one of the biggest encouragers to come on board. Colin passed away unexpectedly in December 2014 which has left us with a huge void in our lives. We would never have embarked on this journey without Colin's encouragement and support. Together we constructed the business getting support from local business people.

What was your first entrepreneurial experience?

We ran a very small business for 20 years. I was in banking and Darren was working in the water industry but we also sold performance car parts and Darren built engines and did a lot of mechanical performance in the backyard.

We had a good understanding of where we were going before we launched out in a big way. With the Lamattina team, the initial team that he drove for, he actually prepared the car, trained the crew, built the race trailer and put everything together. So in some ways, before we took it upon ourselves, we had already done it previously and had that experience behind us.

How would you define success?

In our situation, it's not financial success because it's been very expensive for us but success is winning and we are a very low budget team compared to those that we race against. We're racing against people that turn over a million dollars a week in their business and our success is by beating them.

We are four times Australian Champions now and have won more events than anybody in Australia ever has. So to us, we're very successful.

What's been your most satisfying moment in business?

Without a doubt, winning that first championship as Darren Morgan Racing was the most satisfying moment.

Being able to achieve our number one goal within a few years, which included racing against Americans and defeating them. To achieve that is huge in our industry.

Do you pack up your cars and transport them all around Australia?

We have a semi-trailer which takes our race vehicle to wherever it needs to be. We've travelled to Perth and to Cairns for a half day display for a sponsor. The truck driver takes about three days to get to Perth and our crew comes from all over Australia.

We initially had a crew that was all based in Mildura. It is such a big commitment so the crew has to be quite flexible but people come and go all the time. In our current crew, which we've had for several years, two are based in Perth, one is based in Sydney, one is in Albury, one is in Melbourne and then the balance of them are in Mildura.

How do you coordinate the team with them being spread around Australia?

At some point in the year, they all come back to Mildura and may be here for a week working together and preparing the car but most of the preparation is done by Darren, Ben (our engineer) and the Mildura crew. Together, they get as much done as they can before a race.

We generally get to a race meeting a few days before the race and the rest of the crew will do what needs to be done for racing. They may test the car and then we'll have a few days in between where the boys can work together and because they are very knowledgeable in their areas and we've worked with them for a long time now so they're well trained in what needs to be done and very efficient.

Because they don't work together all the time and they come together at a high pressure point, do you find you have any conflicts between them?

We're very structured in how our team works. Everyone has designated roles and they stick to their roles. Our engineer is the crew chief and we also have a care chief, Rodney. Everybody is well aware of what they have to do. Even though many of them can do someone else's job, they don't do those jobs unless there is an emergency and someone gets hurt or they have to swap out. They will always stick to exactly what they have to do. The reason we do that is because it's such a high pressure situation and it can be dangerous if you get in anyone else's way.

Occasionally there can be small conflicts between crew members but they are a great bunch of people and have never had any real conflict.

> *"Follow your vision and your heart, stay true to yourself always and keep your finger on the pulse. Get a good support group around you."*
>
> **Kathy Ross**

How do you find those people that have that passion?

The crew we have now have all come from previous drag racing relationships, as in they've worked for other people or they have been involved with drag racing and that's what they've wanted to do. We met our tuner, Ben, the engineer who works for us, when he was a little boy and he raced Junior Dragster which is what my children race. When he got to year 10 he wanted to do work experience with us so he came and stayed with us for two weeks. He actually went to Perth on a racing trip with us although at that time Darren was driving for the previous team.

Then, when Ben finished Year 12, he wanted to take a gap year before he went to university and asked us if we would be interested in taking him on for a year. So we did, and when he went to university he came back to Mildura nearly every weekend and every holiday and worked for us. Now he's employed full time, since completing his university degree two years ago.

Generally, those people who approach us are very passionate about racing. Sometimes we've had people come and go because they come in and realise how much hard work it is then decide it's not for them.

They don't realise how hard it is. In our situation at a race meeting, once we've finished an event it may be midnight or later that night, we then have three hours of packing up before we can celebrate. It's a very tough environment.

In order to be competitive we have an emergency supply of every single component on the car. The only thing we don't take to a race meeting, which we would if we could fit it in, is a spare chassis. We had an incident in 2008 where Darren crashed a car. It was the only time he's had an accident, but if we'd had the chassis that was sitting at home in the trailer, he would have been racing again the next day. We didn't have it so he couldn't. We have six engines because for a race meeting we do six passes and in order to do that you really need to have six engines in case you blow them up. So we take everything that we require to do six passes, no matter what happens.

How long would it take to replace a motor if it did blow up?

For each pass that the car goes down the track, the car comes back and the engine is actually pulled apart to check for damage and then the crew replace it depending on what happened. They may replace the entire engine or they may replace parts but they always put on a fresh pair of heads and new spark plugs plus refresh the supercharger. We have an hour and a half in the race schedule to do that and the boys need that time to complete it.

What advice would you give college students who want to do something related to a racing team and just follow that sort of idea?

The best way to get into it is to follow the race teams around if you can. We've had plenty of young men approaching us, wanting to come out and have a bit of a look. We work with the Albury Wodonga motorsport program at TAFE and they bring a lot of students to a lot of our meetings and they'll work with us for a few events and they may come back to Mildura and work at the workshop for a week or two to gain experience in the field. There's no specific motorsport program in Australia that covers Top Fuel, so the only way for people to get experience or get involved is to actually meet a team and try and get onboard.

What is the difference between Top Fuel and other types of motorsport?

With Top Fuel, after each pass the engine must be pulled down. It's the only type of motorsport in the world where you have to pull the engine apart in one and a half hours and put it back together again. There are others where you might have a look at things but not actually physically pull it completely apart and redo it. It's the only motorsport that does that.

To win an event, driving skills are obviously required and very important because listening to the engine and knowing what's going to happen and getting your foot off the pedal so it doesn't blow up is really vital and very strategic. The actual building of the engine and tuning it to get down the race track, depending on weather conditions is where races are won or lost.

But engine skill is far more important than anything else; the building of the engine and making sure that everything is 100% right every time.

On a weekend we would do six passes, three on each day. We have done four in one day but that's really pushing it. That's really too hard for the team but we have been in situations where we had to do that.

A day in the life at the race track, what would that consist of?

At all events our team comes together in the days preceding the event and we all stay together in the same accommodation. There is a lot of preparation involved at the track before an event. We eat all of our meals together which I either prepare or organise.

Early on race day the crew head to the track and commence preparations for the day. They need to put the car together which may involve rebuilding engines, grinding clutch discs and putting the clutch together, building the supercharger, checking the vehicle for cracks or problems. Our crew chief needs to assess the weather to determine what tune up he will put in later in the day.

If it's the second day of racing, they'll have work to do from the previous day so they'll be working on the things they damaged the day before to make sure they're ready for the next race meeting. Because they are not all living in Mildura, they do as much maintenance as they can when they're all together.

Darren will have numerous publicity engagements during the day.

I coordinate our meals for the day as well as the merchandising.

Generally, at a race meeting, if we have corporate guests and depending on how many guests, I may hire a caterer or may do the meals myself but if we have no corporate guests, I do all the meals. So, I prepare what I'm going to have and have my shopping list ready and have ordered or booked what I need to well in advance.

Straight after lunch, the boys will generally start the race car to make sure it's working as it should. After each rebuild of the engine they have to start the car to make sure that it runs well and they also need to check the timing.

Then there is about an hour before they go out to race. The first race is generally at 4:00pm or 5:00pm and then it's full on until the end of the night, so every hour and a half to two hours, they're back on the race track and in between they are just working flat out. If it's boiling hot it doesn't matter.

I'm usually running around making sure the crew are hydrated, that they are wearing what they should be, that our corporate guests are comfortable and happy, that Darren is signing autographs and looking after his guests. I also assist Darren with packing the parachutes and ensure all safety equipment is where it should be when it is needed. On the race track I have the job of assisting Darren into his safety equipment and making sure the parachute pins are pulled out at the appropriate time.

Whilst race weekends are extremely busy, the majority of the work is really conducted prior to the event back in the workshop. Attention to detail is so important and ensures we keep on top of things on race day.

> *"Just do what you need to do, to get what you need to get done."*
>
> *Lynette Gray*

How many other cars would be in a competition on race day?

In Top Fuel, there's normally eight to ten at an Australian National Drag Racing Association (ANDRA) event. But on the day there are probably be between 200 and 600 different vehicles, depending on the event in several different categories.

How has drag racing affected your family life and what are the benefits and some of the challenges?

The benefits for us as our children have been growing up, (we have three teenagers) is the family unity that we have and that our children have got very good life skills.

They can catch a plane to anywhere by themselves. Our eldest son spends most weekends in the shed and he has formed good friendships with the older men who work on the team as well as have a vital role on the team.

It has just instilled really good values in our children and they have made such wonderful friends at the races. We've been all over Australia, which is really fantastic. With the children racing themselves, it has it has created a strong bond in the family unit that we may not have had without racing.

The downside is that we're busy all the time and it has been difficult when the children have been studying in their senior years. Trying to juggle school commitments, maintenance and racing commitments it can be very difficult at times.

What's your greatest fear and how do you manage that fear?

For me personally, financial issues are my biggest fear. I am a very reserved person financially so making the decision to go into this was a very big step for me. I worked in the bank for 15 years and I am very conservative. It's very hard for me to get my head around borrowing or spending a lot of money. Making sure our lifestyle for our children is secure is really the most important for me so I'm most fearful of losing that.

The other great fear that I have is that something happens to Darren. When he first started driving and it was decided that's what he was going to do I said to him at the time, "It's your choice to do this because you want to do it and I want you to do it but be prepared that if something happens to you and you're in a wheelchair, I'm not going to look after you."

I told him that but it's actually not true because I would but I wanted him to be aware that if he was taking this risk with his life, he mustn't expect me to hang around for the rest of my life.

He has had one bad accident but he didn't get a scratch, he was perfectly okay. It's a very safe sport compared to water skiing or other motorsports.

What would you consider to be your greatest achievement?

I think my greatest achievement is being as successful as we have been with our wins because we come from the country. When we first started racing, there were a lot of naysayers who told us that there was no way we were ever going to be successful because, "One, you are from the country and two, you have no money so how can you possibly think you can compete against us?" but we've beaten them all many times. That would be our greatest achievement.

The key elements I guess are having the passion, Darren and I are not people that give up on anything, having that force behind us that we're not going to be losers and having key people to do the right things and play the roles that they play.

Do you believe there's some sort of pattern or formula to being successful?

I think there probably is and we're probably still learning that but I do think that if you don't have passion, then you just can't be successful because if you can't push yourself beyond what is normally expected, then you can never be successful.

What is the one thing you wished you knew before you started?

I am currently studying Bachelor of Business, Accounting – majoring in Management and Marketing at university and I wish that I'd done it earlier. The concepts that are coming out now, although I was doing them, I didn't understand why I was doing them and I think I would have been able to make better business decisions had I had that knowledge earlier.

What do you do to market your business?

What we've found as we've progressed is that in order to market, we have to look at different ways other than just putting a sticker on a racing car. That's not what businesses want, so we're really into the promotion of corporate days or corporate hospitality.

We're finding what a lot of businesses want is to give something to their clients. This has been very successful for us, where they bring 100 people to the races and we'll give them a day where they can actually be in the pits with us.

Drag racing is the only motorsport in Australia where people can actually be in the pits at all times so the clients come and we have a marquee next to our pit area and they can watch the boys working all day and they can take photographs and interact with us and we provide a meal, nibbles and drinks as well as merchandise to make the guests feel part of the team. We have a photographer take photos of them which they get on the day and they have photographs with Darren or they can have photos with promotional girls.

We went to Cairns to a Bunnings Festival and took the racing car up there and started it for them. They even had a famous singer singing and clowns at the festival. We also do things like take the racing car up to agricultural shows and motoring shows. Darren has been to many sorts of events with the car but he will also do public speaking at events. He is a lecturer at TAFE and teaches automotive and motorsport subjects but at the moment he's in the process of doing instruction videos so that our sponsors can use them for online training.

He recently completed an instruction video for XForce Exhaust where he demonstrates how to install a new exhaust on your car. It's that sort of brand ambassador type of thing. We do data collection at the events like the Cairns Bunnings Festival. We've done a lot of data collection over the years. We went to the Bathurst V8 supercars event and displayed our vehicle and a burnout for them on the race track on race day. We've had thousands of people come and see the race car during these events. There is always lots of customer interaction so we do a lot more than just put stickers on race cars.

How did you get involved with Upper Middle Bogan TV program?

The writers of Upper Middle Bogan obviously came up with the idea. They researched drag racing and they researched Top Fuel. We're currently one of the only Victorian teams in the competition. At Easter in Mildura we have a very big motorsport weekend and the writers came to Mildura and found us.

We actually had our car on display at a Motor Show and Shine for the weekend and they came and spoke to us and told us that this was their idea and asked if we would mind if they observed us. So they did that and then about 12 months later they contacted us again and said they'd written the show and got approval from the ABC and asked if we would like to be involved. Yeah! In the first series, we had to use two Top Fuel vehicles and we had to change bodies and pretend to be several different teams.

So we were swapping bodies and putting our blue body on and then a red body and did all this mucking around. We flew the team in from all over Australia to actually run the vehicle. We had two vehicles on the start line at the same time, Darren in one and an actor pretending to be the driver was sitting in the other car while it was running. Our crew disconnected the clutch so the car couldn't go anywhere. They had removed the linkage between the back wheels and the engine so it couldn't actually move.

In the second series they used our children's junior dragster as well as our racecar. They used our son, Rory as the stunt driver which was very exciting for a 12 year old. They needed two other junior dragsters so they used our crew chief Ben's step brother's cars. It was a lot of fun and a really fantastic experience for all of us.

Darren also built a two-seater Top Fuel dragster last year for a man in Queensland and it's the only one in the world that you can go for a ride in. Gup purchased it from Darren, he actually runs Power Cruise Promotions, and he runs 20 something events a year at different locations across Australia, New Zealand and America. The car was just something he wanted to do because it was fun. Darren drives it for him as a promotional tool for the Powercruise events. It's a really good marketing tool and can be used it to entice our sponsors.

We also have a top fuel race simulator which gets attached to the racing car. You can be sitting in a real racing car and drive it like an arcade game. That's a top attraction at some events because people can jump in and have a bit of a drive and it tells you how fast you supposedly went. We come up with a lot of different promotional ideas which are not just racing ideas.

It's really all about the adrenaline isn't it?

To win a race like that, what sort of speeds do you do?

Our speed is 500 kilometers an hour. Each pass is 4.40 or 5.00 seconds, 4.41 is the Australian record at the moment. A really good run is 4.5 seconds.

Who has been your greatest inspiration?

Graeme Cowen without a doubt is our inspiration. He's been the Australian champion who has raced in America and Darren actually raced with him in America. He is our mentor and our inspiration for wanting to win at all costs.

When you grow up, what do you want to be?

I always wanted to be a mummy and I guess one day I want to be a nanny. What is really the most important thing in my life are my children and making sure they have the best opportunities in life.

Where do you see yourself and your business in ten years or twenty years?

Our idea is that we'll have a business that our children can be involved in and that they will literally take over, not that it will be an empire but we have something that our children are proud to say that they are involved with too. We've been faced with some great challenges over the last few years but if you believe in yourself, you can do anything.

CHAPTER 4

Kathy Ross

CEO
iCOS,
Auckland New Zealand

CHAPTER 4

Kathy Ross
CEO
iCOS,
Auckland New Zealand

Kathy Ross is CEO of iCOS Live, a software company for transport logistics that allows online bookings and interaction between customers and transport operators in real time located in New Zealand. Kathy is an Entrepreneur and Visionary whose concept of online booking within the transport industry was light years ahead of its time when the company first designed the product in 2009. She has triumphed through many trials and tribulations including divorce and the death of her partner who took all the passwords and security ID's to his grave. She has financially single-handedly brought this company through recessions and good times to what it represents today.

Just recently she was selected to be part of a delegation led by the Auckland City Mayor to attend a Tripartite Summit in Los Angles, for her "Innovation in Transport".

What ignited the spark in you to start a new business adventure and how did the idea of your business come about?

To be honest, we actually started two business ventures. The first one was during the share market crash in 1988 -1989 when my partner, Chris Grace, returned from Australia where he was working for an international freight forwarder and he could not get a job in New Zealand.

He started a freight forwarding business and also started writing a computer program to help him run that business. He was developing it in Windows 2. Yes! Can you believe it, Windows 2?

Microsoft didn't have an office in NZ then, just an agent. One of their sales reps approached Chris to see if he would write an importing package for a large New Zealand chemical company as they were looking for a PC version as at that time there were only mainframe versions. He was one of the first to release a package in Windows 2 in NZ.

As we both had an international freight forwarding background, when I saw the results of what he had created I said to him, "With your brains and my personality we should go into business together" and that's what we did.

Chris named the software iCOS which stood for Integrated Cargo Operating System. He developed software packages for the transport and related industries over the next 13 years.

In 2003, Chris had a massive heart attack and he passed away and my world crashed in around me in more ways than one. My family wanted me to close the doors and walk away but I felt I had a responsibility to:

a) The customers

b) The staff

So I hung in there and carried on the best I could. I wanted to be in control of my own destiny rather than going back to work for someone else.

I had been working with the importing and exporting clients and Chris with the domestic transport ones. Soon after Chris's death, an Australian competitor with a transport software package came into the New Zealand market and paid me a visit. He suggested I hand over my clientele as he was going to take them anyway.

Well, that was like a red rag to a bull for me.

I advised him, "With what customer base I have left, I will continue to do my best to support them, thank you, but no thank you..." It only made me more determined to keep going.

He was true to his word and slowly, one by one, many of the transport customers used his software. Things became very tight and I was struggling personally as well as financially.

I had several offers of help from men in the industry but very soon alarm bells rang; they were looking for a free ride at my expense.

It was hard work trying to establish myself and be taken seriously.

After all, the transport sector is very male dominated and today there still aren't that many women figureheads but it is changing. I have been told that women truck drivers are highly regarded but a few years back they weren't even considered.

To be honest, if it had not been for my supportive Aunt Kitty who lived next door to me, I don't know how I would have kept going, let alone keep those doors open. She was always available to lend me an ear and a guiding hand even though she was in her 90s. An ex infant mistress teacher and very much for women in the work force, she would wait up until I got home each day, often after 8pm, and we would run over the day.

She was very spiritual and looked at everything positively. She was an inspiration not only in my life but many others too.

After much thought I decided to change tack and come in under the radar. The Australian company was targeting the big boys so I started visiting the smaller transport operators in the 5-20 truck range. Most companies were family operations with Mum and Dad starting out. I felt I could really relate to these people.

Many of their stories were similar in:-

Dad had worked for the big boys but didn't like the way they did business so they followed their own dreams of providing a better service to their clients, convincing Mum to mortgage their house and buy a truck and as the business grew, another and another.

Often Dad was driving a truck, Mum had the job of doing the accounts and taking care of the kids - dragging them to the depot during school holidays or when they were sick as she needed to be hands on too.

The accounts often consisted of a shoebox filled with dirty con-notes, which had been stomped on or had coffee spilt over them.

They were illegible, so she didn't know whether the charge amount was $2,500 or $25 and more often than not, the lesser amount was charged out.

Dad wore boots and shorts and wrote on his arms and legs. Tired at the end of the day, he would often forget to copy the information from his body parts before taking a shower and the information was lost.

He would stay up late pondering, "Did I pick that job up?" or "Did I deliver that piece," etc. etc.

What I found was that they all had several things in common. They were busy working in the business but they never had time to work on the business. They were buried under paperwork, causing loss of revenue which they weren't aware of.

> *"If I could start again I would actually document more because I'd have a paper trail. These were the ideas running through my head before I walked into this situation, this is how I felt in this situation and this is how I feel after the situation.*
>
> *It's hard to remember everything and you often make the same emotional mistakes again and again."*
>
> **Eleni Mitakos**

If they didn't have anyone to help with the children then they couldn't take sick leave or a holiday for that matter and it was hardly a life, working 24/7.

One company I visited was exactly as I describe above but she had to wait until her husband had time to sit down and go through the paper dockets so they could be priced out because all the rates were in his head.

The problem was that he couldn't remember what he had charged the last time so invariably credit notes had to be issued – more paper, double handling.

Software was not something he was interested in; he had it all in his head so he didn't need help. "What if something happens to you?" I asked but to no avail.

A month later, this man died of a heart attack and it brought it all back home to me. Chris held so much information in his head including passwords to software modules that to this day I have not been able to access.

We were still trading in 2008-2009 when the recession hit NZ and so many transport companies were beginning to fall, both large and small. Over the Christmas break I was out on the water, sitting alone on the back of the boat and thinking about these companies, my own company, and wondering what future there was in store for us all and I said "God, there has to be a better way." Then an epiphany happened and the message was clear - *redevelop the software into an Internet Cargo Operating System.*

I was compelled to go snorkelling, something I wasn't keen on doing and screeds of information poured into my head, I had to get out of the water and jot it all down, pages upon pages. I was so excited and couldn't wait to get back to work to share my experience with the team.

I advised them, "We are going to create an Internet Transport Management System which will allow our clients and their customers to book online just like internet banking. This way it gives the owners and the staff, especially if they are working mums, the ability to work from home if the children are sick or take them on holiday because they would be able to access the program via the internet.

We would host the software so they didn't have to spend thousands of dollars on servers which could be washed away in a flood, destroyed in an earthquake or burnt in a fire. We would help them to stop pushing paper around but even better, get our clients and customers to send the jobs in electronically from their internal systems via EDI.

We would create a way so that they wouldn't lose a docket and plug the revenue leakage that they didn't even know they had.

We employed a Dot Net programmer who worked with Keith Russell, who is our transport development manager, and who is still with us today.

I had no money, just a vision and the banks wouldn't lend me any, there was a recession going on and it wasn't like the business was booming back then. A year later we had only completed the basic foundations.

Again it was my aunty who was there for me – she funded us, keeping the doors open so that we could make this vision a reality. It wasn't easy and many a time I couldn't even afford to buy a bottle of milk as I went without pay and put my life on hold.

It was hard on my family as my kids felt like I was always at work, never at home and friends all but gave up on me as there was no time or money for a social life.

Jesse Morgan joined our team and the system went from strength to strength. The vision grew bigger and bigger with their collective ideas and I made statements like, "I want to take this product global, I want mass penetration of the transport sector by linking one transport company to another and another so we can deliver a complete electronic paperless solution globally." Imagine!!!

We approached Xero online accounting to use their system as the back end so we could totally focus on the operational side which meant both systems were hosted in the cloud. We do have medium sized businesses that have their own accounting system and we have interfaced with them but Xero is a true integration so the products have become one.

There was a lot of revenue pilferage going on during the recession – by receivers of goods making statements that they had not received them.

One of my customers told me that a pallet of butter was delivered to a supermarket but the next day that same supermarket said they hadn't received the goods. The signature was illegible on the docket and the driver hadn't recorded the name so they had no option but to pay out the claim. These stories grew so we asked ourselves how we could help these operators to overcome this. Expensive PDA's were out for most so we developed our own Android App calling it iCOS GO which offered an affordable mobility solution using smart devices to send job data to the trucks. The drivers could inform the back office of each step of the freight's movements, when they picked up and offloaded and when they had obtained a signature and signee name for proof of delivery with the system date and time stamp and display this back to our client's customers. It certainly transformed freight tracking.

It wasn't long before I was paid a visit from a big boy saying, "How dare you develop this system, you are giving these small to medium operators the ability to compete with us; in fact they can offer more to their clients than we can and we have spent thousands of dollars on our internal systems."

"Fantastic, I have achieved what I set out to do," I replied.

What motivates you?

I love helping people; it gives me so much personal satisfaction.

I have a passion and desire to see this vision become a great success. I tell stories all the time now about all the wonderful things that have happened to my customers with their bottom lines increasing by 33% in six months without new customers and having a life they never had before – like you, Lynette Gray. You were telling me the story of how you had not been able to take a holiday in 15 years, let alone write this book.

Putting iCOS LIVE in place, integrated with Xero, and enabled you to do that. Refer to Kwik 'n' Kool on our website www.icoslive.com.

How do you generate new ideas?

I get inspiration when I'm just being quiet out on the water. Our brilliant team and our customers are always coming up with creative ideas. If we listen to their needs and can make their lives better, we are half way there.

What has been your most satisfying moment in business?

Hearing the wonderful stories about how iCOS LIVE has changed lives.

There are some really good ones:-

Bob was a one man band and grew to six owner drivers, sold out to a big boy and went on to live the life of BIG WEDNESDAY, the batch, the holiday etc.

Your story, Lynette, about taking your family on holiday. (Refer to the Bonus Chapters on the Women In Workboots website for this story)

Another one is where a company put our system in but wouldn't listen to me and didn't use Xero, didn't use tablets in the trucks, didn't get customers booking online and didn't receive electronic jobs from their customers. They didn't have an end to end solution and they went into liquidation still buried under the paper while working in the business not on it. The brilliant outcome of that story is that they are now promoting our product and telling operators their story.

"If only we had listened to Kathy!"

I will never be Mother Theresa or Florence Nightingale but if I can help these small to medium operators in some way then I've achieved something in my lifetime.

"Impossible just means that you have not found the right solution yet. There are many ways to get the right result."

Lynette Gray

How do you find people to bring into your business that truly care about your business?

No one will have the passion or feel about things the way you do because they haven't put their life on the line or mortgaged their house to make it happen.

But lead by example, always be positive and always allow people to contribute. One of the things that Chris taught me is that you cannot put anyone in a box, particularly programmers.

When I interview people for a job, I say to them, "If you want to be in a structured environment where you sit in a little cubicle and you're told, 'Write that line of code,' don't come and work here. If you want to come here and think, 'Wow, I am part of this, I can contribute' and bounce ideas around with the team putting forward your creative ideas, whiteboard marker in hand, coffee in the other, then there is room on the iCOS bus for you."

What would you say are the top 3 skills needed to be successful at what you love doing and how far are you willing to go to succeed?

Passion, tenacity and confidence within yourself.

It's having that *tenacity* to keep going because when you're passionate and you love doing what you're doing, you wake up in the morning and you want to get out of bed. It's a new exciting day!

The first thing I do when I wake up is say, "Good morning, world. Thank you for another day. I am one with the universe and the universe is one with me. Thank you for my beautiful family. Thank you for all the people I can help today. Thank you for all the rewarding sales that will come through our door today. Thank you to my creative, supportive, wonderful team. Thank you. I am so grateful for everyone and everything in my life."

What have been some of your failures and what have you learned from them?

After Chris's death I felt so alone and vulnerable. I abdicated in some areas and very soon the vultures were trying to take control. Big mistake.

iCOS LIVE is my baby. I will not take my finger off the pulse and I won't let anybody take control until I'm ready to release it.

What is your greatest fear?

Myself – my limiting beliefs.

How do you manage that fear?

I talk myself into trusting the universe. It'll be alright.

What do you think is the greatest achievement and single most important reason for your success?

Firstly, I am a mother. I have three wonderful children whom I adore, Tracy, David and Katrina and now I have 8 beautiful grandchildren one of which is Jamie who now works as part of our development team.

My daughter Tracy has been an amazing support and runs the finances with an iron fist; bless her. David joined the business in sales and is our South Island manager.

Then my next greatest achievement is iCOS LIVE. Developing this I found myself, the missing piece of ME.

How has being an entrepreneur affected your family life?

Ask my kids this question they will say, "What family life? Certainly in the early days I didn't have one.

It hasn't been easy that's for sure but that comes down to limiting one's self and one's thinking and lack of money. Once you empower yourself the money flows and things do become easier.

Looking back, what's one thing you wish you understood about entrepreneurship before you ever got started?

You don't have to have a degree, I didn't have one, so I started to believe comments that were made by certain males that I shouldn't be doing what I was. Its rubbish, you just have to have total faith in yourself. No self-doubt, just follow the dream. Money sure helps all the same.

If you could offer a first time entrepreneur one piece of advice, what would it be?

Follow your vision and your heart, stay true to yourself always and keep your finger on the pulse. Get a good support group around you.

It's amazing the number of people who have come into my life and believed in and encouraged me. Denis Hanley has been an amazing support person who I met through my lady lawyer. I don't know what I would have done without my wonderful lady bank manager. I am very grateful to them all.

What is your favourite book?

"The Secret" by Rhonda Byrne. I read this over and over.

Ever since I was young I've questioned, "What is my reason for being here? What is the point of it all?

Why am I here?

There has got to be more to life than this."

I married very young, almost straight out of school and we lived in the country. It was a good family life but I just felt something was missing. I worked part time in various jobs and ran a family. Still, I felt there had to be more so I eventually moved on, taking my children back to the city to find a career as I wanted to make something of myself. I started in sales first with a medical care company and then the international freight forwarding. I eventually became the NZ manager for an Australian company, it was very exciting and I loved that job. Chris and I got together and a whole new chapter of my life began.

Now I know that I am an instrument for the universe to work through and help others see and learn; we are unlimited beings.

Mike Dooley, New York Times bestselling author, speaker and entrepreneur in the philosophical New Thought movement states "Thoughts become things."

It's so true. Leave the negative stuff behind and focus only on the positive and the world is a much better place and give gratitude for all that you have and more follows.

Where do you see yourself and your business in 10 years?

Transport operators are finding it tough in Australia right now with another recession looming, so the first step is getting across the ditch to help them too.

I'd like to see iCOS LIVE become a global company, even if it has someone else at the helm.

I wish to leave a legacy behind and for my kids to say to their kids, "The lady that transformed freight tracking." Your grandmother was a workaholic when we were growing up but she always put us first and they do say that now. Look what she achieved because she believed she could make a difference. She was very passionate about what she set out to do - albeit late in life.

I left my run a little late, so I guess I will personally be well retired in 10 years. I trust that I'll be alive to see how the company has grown and the rewards that have come from all the hard work for my partner Paul and myself as well as my children and their children and the difference it's made to people's lives.

CHAPTER 5

Eleni Mitakos

Galmatic
2013 Telstra Business Womens' Awards Nominee

CHAPTER 5

Eleni Mitakos

Galmatic

2013 Telstra Business Womens' Awards Nominee

Eleni Mitakos has a passion for driving and tinkering with cars, since buying her first vintage car as a teenager. That car was a 1956 Holden FE, which had neither side view mirrors, nor seatbelts, but she thought it made her the coolest gal in town! So in love with her first car and navy overalls on, she was eager to get her hands greasy!

So 13 years later, with that dream still in mind, she left the corporate world behind and established Galmatic - an old fashioned service orientated car care garage; hands on, friendly and trustworthy. Since then she has been featured in over 20 publications and was a 2013 Telstra Business Womens' Awards Nominee. She has extensive experience in corporate training and program design in a variety of industries and is fully qualified to deliver a full range of Performance Driving programs.

So with 25 years' of driving both old and new cars, and 15 years in the entertainment industry, she has devoted a lifetime of teaching and training and a desire to introduce other women to the fun and enjoyment of being car and road savvy.

What was the spark that made you start and decide on this business venture and how did the idea for your business come about?

The idea actually came from my early 20s, in a Rockabilly Rock 'n Roll Sydney scene. I used to have an old '50s car and my girlfriend also had a '50s car and the group we liked had a '50s cars and we were watching a Rock 'n' Roll band in our big full petticoat skirts and the boys were outside tinkering with their cars and we just thought, "There's something we're not comfortable with about this." Even though we liked the era and the vintage clothing, being born in the decade we were born in and the fact that we were watching a band or the boys were playing with cars, we thought was leading us back into the '50s just a little bit.

So we were joking that we needed something for women to have a car culture and in the background there was the greatest movie playing with lyrics to a song. They included hydromatic, automatic and systematic and that's how the name "Galmatic" started when I was about 21, I think, but I did nothing with it until I was 33.

Typically, women are not associated with cars, unless they're the partner of a male that's in the mechanical industry, a mechanic or their husband or partner is a racing car driver. It just isn't a culture for women, they are usually more worried about how cute their handbags look or the way they look or stuff like that.

But we don't associate women with their vehicle. Maybe they'll go and buy pink number plates or a fancy penny to put on their dashboard. The more I thought about it the more I realised how frightening it is, especially after you become a mother and put your brand new baby in a car seat and bringing them home from the hospital. Then you realise that this is a machine that can very easily travel at 160 kilometres an hour.

At no point do you really notice that, as a culture or a community, we are concerned about our females in cars. We are happy to supply you with a brand new "beep-beep Barina" jump in, drive off and go, "Oh, thank goodness I don't have to drive her around anymore. Oh my goodness." We are happy to put them into vehicles with them having very little, if any, understanding of how a motor vehicle works.

So, the idea was always there but the springboard was giving birth to my own daughter and it started off very simply and has grown organically into what Galmatic is today.

How did you generate new ideas?

Having originally worked in corporate, one of the skills I learnt was to think of the big picture. I did know different avenues of income streams that I wanted and I did have a big picture and I knew the things that I definitely did not want to do and one of those things I never wanted was investors.

So how have your entrepreneurial motivations changed since you started Galmatic?

In the beginning I had that delusional state for some time, almost like The Bold and The Beautiful. As I've gone through the years I've realised that you actually do have a hand in more than you want to, until you get to a place where you can afford to hire people. I've now focused more on how I can grow the business, always with new products and new ideas and how I can drive them into the market place.

Whereas before, all I saw myself doing was the training. It's very common for people when you're a technician or you have the training background and of course are a little extroverted because I find teaching comes very easily for me and people find me entertaining. I kept doing all the classes, which is good in one sense because people like it, but it means that you are always chasing the hourly dollar and you're also always focusing on the actual tools of the trade, not on growing the actual business.

Being from a migrant background, my father was a young concrete farm worker and my mum worked. One of the things mum always used to say was, "Oh goodness," because there were always dirty boots on the back doorstep and she was always instructing me, "Never marry a man that leaves dirty boots on the back doorstep," because their idea of dirty boots means you're working for the hour, the hourly dollar. Dirty boots means you can't use your mind, you're using your body for manual labour, and I really laughed because I still keep boots today. My mum died when I was young so as my little token to her, I always leave my boots on the back doorstep and I just think, "There you go, Mum, it's okay, they're my boots."

As I get older I've come to realise how entrenched a lot of the business or work ideals have been in our minds since we were children. It's what we observed, what we were taught and how we were brought up to see business.

I went to school and university but there were far more traditional ways that women could make money. I'm finding cultural traditions, as I was born in the '70s, meant very different ways of working in those days. I am a female empowering women but I really want to make sure that I can show my children, who are both females, the life balance in this and that there's more enjoyment in life.

I'm able to financially support myself and my family but also be a member of the community and a good mother. It's good to be able to incorporate all those things.

I found that as part of that entrepreneurial journey, the more you think outside the box the more you really start thinking of how you can contribute on a daily basis to not just your local community but to each and every single woman that drives in Australia.

What would you say are the top skills needed to be successful at what you love doing and how far are you going to go in order to succeed?

The three things for me are:-

1. Have a really clear idea of what your skills are. Really know what you're good at, not just technically but emotionally as well.
Really knowing what your trigger points are, knowing where your sensitivities are and knowing where your strengths are.
"Look, this may not go quite right but I'm not going to take it to heart because of that one thing."

2. Be very clear about what you want from the business and not just financially. Sometimes when you make business plans or when you talk to other people, the main discussion point for them is how much money you're going to make or the financial goals.

As a female, especially if you have or are going to have children, you need to know your goals, where you want to work, how often you want to work, how much you're going to travel, how much time you want to commit to the school or community and how much you want to do with your friends.

"You can teach skills but you can't teach attitude."

Lynette Gray

As women, we tend to just take on every chore and add it to the end of the chore list to the point that we're only sleeping three hours a night because physically, we can only do so many things. And the whole reason why we started the business has gone out the window because we just can't keep doing any more.

Think really clearly about what you want from the business.
3. Be able to take people's advice and take the good bits out of it and not offend them by ignoring the rest of it.

You have to know what you can take from people without insulting them because at the end of the day, you do want people to be involved and giving you ideas, otherwise it's just you working in one room and bouncing your own ideas against the wall or you just chase your tail trying to do what everyone suggests.

If you had the chance to start out again, what would you do differently?

If I had the chance to start over again, the first thing I would do would be to waste less money on marketing and on the things that I thought would make us money. I know when I started, I was like, "Okay, I'm going to do this, this and this," and I would either easily put money into it so I could drive it or I would have left it to grow organically that little bit longer, so I could see what did and didn't work.

I would have focused more on who I hired to do our training because we're all females. Unfortunately, like it or not, when you work with females, family does come into it. Originally I focused too much on finding people who knew about the mechanics of cars, whereas now it's more about, here's what we do. We have a system and they have to follow the system. The biggest marketing tool that has worked the best for us is word of mouth.

What are some of your failures and what have you learned from them?

A lot of the time when working with big business, you have five or six meetings. I soon discovered that my time is valuable and the money I've made out of this isn't any more than when I just go and teach one of our classes at the school up the road.

Early on in business, I found that I needed to be associated with having worked with the big businesses and I think in the long term that it has been good that we have had those associations but financially, I've made less out of the big business associations than I have out of our little school groups.

What is your greatest fear and how did you manage it?

Whenever I do training in cars, my greatest fear is that something will go wrong, like a tyre would fall off and smack someone in the head. When it comes to business, I think my biggest fear is always the safety component.

I really enjoy how we run our business now, we're doing engine and empowerment and training but my fear is always safety around people.

What would be your greatest achievement and what was the single most important reason for your success?

Over ten thousand women are just that little bit more confident. My goal was to provide a two hour class and leave feeling that someone's life has been changed forever. But everyone that walks away has learnt one thing, they've realised a car is only a machine, so I can touch bits and pieces, I can ask questions and I just started a relationship.

We always think the most important relationship is the one you have with your car because it's the one that drives you to pick up your children from school, it's the one that takes you to job interviews and it's the one that you sing in.

It's a relationship, it's not a transaction and we start relationships that are meaningful ones. Some people have their car for 20 years and some people's relationship with their car lasts much longer than their romantic relationships.

So we want to say, he or she could be one of the main relationships of your life. For a lot of people who don't own any business, property or their own business it's usually the house and car that are the two big investments in their life.

They don't give their car a lot of time, so we start that spark. I think we've taught over 10,000 women how to be a little bit safer behind the wheel.

How has this entrepreneurial lifestyle that you've got, affected your family life?

I have a Boot Log that I take; I photograph my boots and put it on my blog. It's about three years old so my dirty boots have been around Australia. What it allows me to do is do what I need to do, when the time is best for me to do it, not for someone else.

Just last night at 10:30pm my brain was in a creative mood so I proofread my latest set of eBooks whereas in a normal day to day job you have your proofreading done when the proofreading is due. I find that five days before it's due to launch, if I go, "Ah, I'm not quite sure this is right," I don't have to launch it.

It also allows me to have a bit more of a hands-on experience with my girl's school because to me, it was really important that I dropped them off at school and picked them up. I don't have to squash my personality in any way as long as I provide car services and stuff like that, obviously. I can add to teaching things other than just boots but it allows me to blossom in the areas that I can blossom in and I can probably be a little bit more extroverted than a normal work environment would allow me to be.

"I like being a woman, even in a man's world. After all, men can't wear dresses but we can wear the pants."

Whitney Houston

Looking back, what's sort of things do you wish you'd understood about your entrepreneurship before you ever got started?

If I could start again seven years ago, it would be just to actually document more, almost in a journal, because I'd have a paper trail saying this is how I felt, these were the ideas running through my head before I walked into this situation, this is how I felt in this situation and this is how I felt after the situation.

Because it's hard to remember everything you often make the same emotional mistakes when you go into things and for me that would be good, so I could really reference things and say, "Okay, you keep making this same sort of error" or "You keep going over these same things."

I think more journaling because that way you could look back and say, "Okay, you know, do you see the experience I've had?" Because when I look back on the seven years we've had, we have a logo that has grown or we see how Georgie has been in all the photos and we have all these photos of my boots, which is a key because I then remember when there was a crowbar in the photo.

At no point ever, have I noticed that I'm in a very male dominated industry but I get asked that a lot and I find that it's because it's got to do with cars. I wish it was more male dominated but we're all female trainers and we just teach women. Why I think I've never noticed is because it's never been something that I've highlighted to myself to be an issue till now.

What is the best business idea that you'll never use?

It always comes back to training which is like dating in a way. It's a lovely way to meet people. Yeah, so maybe that's the big one. Parker dating.

If you talked to one person from history who would it be and why?

I would love to meet to meet Queen Elizabeth, the virgin Queen Elizabeth, she's Elizabeth the First. I'd like to know how someone like her could be so dominant and rule as a female in those days.
I'd love to meet her. That would be fascinating. I would also love to meet Lady Clicquot, the woman behind Veuve Clicquot? The French champagne. That was started, established and run by a woman and which she technically still runs. She's one of the biggest, richest women of all times, comparatively speaking for that kind of business.

I would love to talk to Madonna, Lady Gaga or even Kylie Minogue. Gold hotpants could not have happened had Madonna not forged the way. And always the decades go past and everything is more acceptable but I think she did quite well back in an era where, you know, that was quite shocking... those bullet bras were just fantastic. Madonna, when she was big, would be fun, historically. Especially Elizabeth, that's really living in a man's world and she almost had to do it by turning into one.

Who has been your greatest inspiration?

I like looking at how people do things and just taking snippets from a lot of people rather than one person. It's being able to take something from different people.

I keep a book, a notebook, so whenever I do any webinars or any sort of training I write it all down into this one book and if you look back through it you will just get bits and pieces of information in there.

I finished university without even ever touching a computer and it wasn't that long ago. I wasn't born in the '50s, I was born in the '70s.

What about the book? What's inspired you most in a book?

I can think of a few but a classic is 'The Amish.' It's old, it's very traditionally written but that to me is great because it really hones in on 99% of the people I know in business who are technicians.

More recently Danielle LaPorte, she's written The Fire Starter Sessions. I really enjoyed reading that as it is all about noting emotional reasons why you're doing something and before you do it, clicking into the emotion you want to feel, so that even if the action doesn't give you the desired raw outcome, the emotion that you wanted behind that action is filled. And if it is, then you fight. It's thinking about emotion. It's kind of like girls getting married and their wedding day. It's got nothing to do with the wedding day, it's how they want to feel on their wedding day. If you asked those brides twenty years later if they would like to get $19,000 back, who wouldn't say, "Oh, yes! What a waste of money" but at the time they wanted to feel like a princess, beautiful, loved and special.

That book is really good at dealing with how you want to feel emotionally. If all you want is to feel pretty, it doesn't cost $19,000. You know, $40 will give you the answer. It's certainly just emotional needs.

So what do you want to do when you grow up?

When I grow up I just want to age gracefully. I don't want to be glorious, I just want to be 80. I'd like to know that when I'm in my coffin there are millions of people crying because I have affected their lives.

Children and teenagers are not embarrassed to let you know, "Oh thanks, I got that" because they're still in that learning phase whereas, when you teach adults, somehow they're too embarrassed to say they need something or that they enjoyed that or try to change. Children are beautiful, they're so open with their playful words, letting you know something was really good.

One of my favourite lessons that we taught was at a convent where the nuns were all over 70 years of age. They could have been born before there were many cars around and they are happily driving but were probably never taught to drive.

One of the things we've never ever had to fight for is the right to drive as a woman but it's one of the areas we've been totally ignorant about from the start. There's no documented history I can find, where women went driving around in a motorcar. Women simply jumped into one and started driving.

It was never a case of, "Oh, you're a woman, you can't drive." I don't know where the modern association comes from because when you look back to the early 1900s there are women driving. Then there was war and obviously women took over wherever they needed to, especially in America during the war era with Rosie the Riveter etc.

Where do you see yourself and your business in 10 or 20 years?

Doing what we do but with every single female in Australia knowing we exist and just waiting for the right time to come and meet us. So all the mums know that's where their daughters are going to go, every school knows that we teach this program and every council knows they can offer the program.

Being able to really touch every female who drives because there are millions learning to drive every year.

My goal is that we reduce the number of young women dying in cars:

a) Because they're passengers but they're happy to sit in the back seat instead of the driver's seat and jump in cars with boys

b) Just so that they know that every time they get behind the steering wheel of a car, it's a privilege, it's not a right and they have their rights as does everyone else.

You don't get in a car with someone that you don't feel comfortable with. There are lifelong consequences.

When we learned how to drive, and with 10 mates in the back of the vehicle, I have clear memories of my next door neighbour, his name was Dan. I was sitting in the back of my dad's ute, with the groceries in an icebox, and he would drive fast so that the icebox would not melt between the shop and home. You can't do that anymore.
I've got lots of photos of me and my boots. I have a very close relationship with my boots.

http://thesebootsaremadeforteaching.blogspot.com.au/

CHAPTER 6

Lynette Gray
Kwik 'n' Kool Refrigerated Couriers
Owner & Operator

CHAPTER 6

Lynette Gray
Kwik 'n' Kool Refrigerated Couriers
Owner & Operator

Member of the Queensland Transport
Association,
Transport Women Australia,
Safe Food Queensland,
The Australian Businesswomen Network,
Qld Rural, Regional & Remote Women's Network,
Surat Basin Enterprise and the Queensland Chamber of Commerce.
Winner of the AIM Queensland Management Excellence Award
Finalist for the Heritage Business Award in the Business and
Professional category.

What ignited the spark in you that started your love for the transport industry?

I got my truck learners the first time when I was seventeen, because mum had her truck licence I would get mine too. I don't even remember not ever having something to do with the transport industry, except for working in a fabric shop fitting out brides and bridesmaids. That was interesting. I could be creative, but I wanted more.

As a kid I would look at the trucks when they drove down the main street of Taroom, especially when the army was moving or when there was mine equipment on the move. We would run down the footpath after school pulling our arm down for the "honk the horn" signal to the drivers. It was always a thrill when we succeeded.

My first job in the transport industry was with Simon National Carriers and I would always watch with keen interest to see how they loaded the road-trains that were headed for Darwin on a Friday night.

Then it was just a natural progression. My parents and my brother had a road-train business, so the discussion was always about this truck or that truck. One thing led to another and when my husband became redundant at Westpac we went out and bought a Pantech truck and started Kwik 'n' Kool.

Tell me about your first entrepreneurial experience as a kid

I don't actually remember being entrepreneurial as a kid. We never had a lot of money and we lived 18km from Taroom on a property. The closest I got to that was a conversation between Mum, Dad and me, "You could bag up all that grain that has fallen on the ground and sell it." "Yep," I could, but I didn't.

I couldn't see who would buy it.

I never really had any entrepreneurial experiences until I was married and I started to look around at other successful people and their lifestyles.

How do you define success?

Success means different things to different people. My definition of success is the feeling of "I've done it" when a goal that has been a major part of your life and your thought process comes to fruition.

Some goals are considered insignificant by some people and gigantic by others but what really matters is that they are your personal goals and when you achieve them it is your *reward* and no one can take that from you.

True success is when you are truly happy in what you are doing.

What has been your most satisfying moment in business?

The most satisfying moments for me would have been when we had a fire in the back of a truck and the steps that we took to get the stock that was on that truck replaced for the customers and the truck back on the road. We were fortunate that the driver opened the doors just before leaving Brisbane and discovered the fire. It would have been a totally different story if he had not had that last stop because he would have been driving up the highway with his back alight.

We contacted all the suppliers and got the customers' stock replaced and sent down another vehicle. The way this was handled meant that some of the customers didn't even realise that we'd had a problem. We just did what we did automatically and didn't think much of it until the next week when one of the suppliers told us of a situation that they had been in where there was a truck roll-over and they were not even told until the next day that their product had been destroyed.

So the most satisfying was the feeling that what we had done was right, even though only a few people knew about it, including the insurance company.

How have your entrepreneurial motivations changed since you first started?

In a word, they have changed massively.

How do you find people to bring into your business that truly care about the business the way you do?

I have found over the years that the people who care more than others are the ones who feel that they are contributing to the success of the business or project. You will never have anyone who will care about it the way you do but you do get close to that when the team is working as one and going in the same direction.

If you had the chance to start your career over again, what would you do differently?

Hold onto my dreams tighter and fight for what I believe in with gusto.

I would have set firm boundaries for myself, my family and my business. The life of my family was so intertwined with that of the employees that the lines between employer and employee became somewhat blurred. I didn't realise that I was unintentionally setting myself up to be a doormat for them.

I know now that you can do more for your employees and give them more opportunities if you keep them at arm's length than if you let them into your personal life.

When you realise that there is a bigger purpose to life, things just begin to fall into place and life begins to synchronise. If I had to do it all over again, I would chase down opportunities and not only for financial reasons.

The mistakes I've made over time have led me to where I am today. I wouldn't change some of those things but if I wanted to start a new business, I would apply the lessons I've learned immediately, so that I could save myself those mishaps in the early days.

What 3 pieces of advice would you give to college students who want to be entrepreneurs?

1. You need to understand that relationships require direction, communication and commitment but above all, trust, to be successful.

2. Don't be afraid to make mistakes but more importantly, learn from those mistakes and don't make the same mistake again.

3. Be a person of integrity, be honest and trustworthy. Have a strong character and don't talk about someone behind their back. Never harass, discriminate, use profanity or tell off-colour jokes.

> *"A man must be big enough to admit his mistakes, smart enough to profit from them, and strong enough to correct them."*
>
> *John C Maxwell*

What is attitude?

The definition of attitude according to the Merriam Webster dictionary is:

"A mental position with regard to a fact or state; a feeling or emotion toward a fact or state."

I think another way to think about attitude is as a mental habit that filters how you perceive the world around you and the actions and behaviours that you are responsible for. A person's attitude is important and has significant bearing on the level of success that you can achieve in life.

Don't fall victim to your own B.S.
Don't talk the talk unless you can walk the walk.
Impress with action not conversation.

What are your ideals?

My ideal is the ability to amalgamate the following so you have a strong, steadfast character.
Be your true self
Be strong in your character
Be happy
Be optimistic
Find new ways of doing things; don't just do things because "that's the way it has always been done"
Make a positive mark in the world
When something doesn't go to plan, as it inevitably will, just find another way to get the desired result

What do you feel is the major difference between entrepreneurs and those who work for someone else?

When you are an entrepreneur these are some of the traits you inherently discover you have:

1. You take charge of your own goals
2. You believe anything is possible
3. Anything worth doing is worth doing well no matter how big or small the project is
4. You have a "what else can I do" or a "now what" attitude
5. Every failure is closer to success
6. You never ever give up
7. Always look for other opportunities
8. You are always asking yourself "How can I do this better?"
9. You have a strong vision

What have been some of your failures and what have you learned from them?

Failure is an interesting word, isn't it. You only fail at something if you give up on it. Edison had 1000 failures when he invented the light bulb and then he had a success. So let me ask you, was it a failure or was it a success??? Imagine if he had given up too soon.

> *"I have not failed. I've just found 10000 ways that won't work."*
>
> *Thomas A. Edison*

What is your greatest fear and how do you manage fear?

As a mother my greatest fear is that something will happen to our boys. So many people told me that you never stop worrying about them, I used to think "Nah, that can't be right." But you know what, you don't stop worrying about them. Pity about what my parents worry about.

What do you consider to be your greatest achievement and what's the single most important reason for your success?

Behind my kids, being my greatest achievement, who are all now successful in their own right in their individually chosen fields. I would have to say the completion of this book. As I struggled through school with a form of Dyslexia never in a million years did I think I would ever write a book.

The journey I have been on for the last few months has been amazing, the encouragement I have received from Global Publishing, Trevor and my closest family and friends has been greatly received when I have had my moments of doubt. I could not have done it without them.

It was good to learn that eventually everyone needs to ask for and receive help. If it's as hard for you as it is for me. It's a skill you need to build up. Here's why:

1. **Sooner or later, you won't have a choice.**
   Even if you've bootstrapped you way to success, even if you're a solopreneur, the day will come when you need to ask someone for help.

2. **Helping benefits the helper.**

   If you've ever helped anyone with anything, you know what I'm talking about. Helping someone generates a warm glow that can make you feel good. How good do you feel when you give to charity?

3. **The next time someone needs your help you'll be able to empathise.**

   You may be the most generous person in the world, but giving help when you've asked for it yourself is completely different from giving it when you never have.

4. **Not needing help is a form of conceit.**

Most of my life I've taken pride in being self-sufficient. But the truth is, that's not a moral strength, it's just vanity. Everyone who's ever succeeded at anything has got help along the way from teachers, relatives, mentors, friends, clients and colleagues.

Asking for help, getting help, offering help, and giving it when it's needed are all ways that we connect and stay connected with each other as human beings. It's precious. And it's worth a lot more than any pride we may have in not needing it.

What is the strangest thing you've ever done?

I don't know about strangest but things that stand out in my mind are from my childhood like my brothers and I would have races through the Brigalow trees on a four wheel motorbike with just enough room between the trees so that you had to give the handlebars just a tweak at the right time to make it through or you would come to a sudden halt.

Another memory is going up the dam bank with Trevor (my now husband) with the dog on the quad bike and at the top we hit a rock which flipped the bike end to end and it rolled down the bank. We were just blessed that the bike went one way and we went the other. I don't know when the dog bailed out and I don't wish to think about what would have happened if it had rolled on top of us.

> *"Getting the direction's the hard part but when I have a direction that I want to follow it might lead me to other things. You've just got to start with something, so make a decision and then flesh it out from there."*
>
> ***Mary Koutalis***

That bike was hours of fun my brother John, the family prankster, thought it would be funny to give me a fright one day. He was driving and he took me down the rubbish dump, which effectively was a hole in the ground dug out by a bulldozer. The bank was quite steep and the bottom that was full of water from the recent rains and he knew that. So through the water he goes flat out. But since he had last been through it we had had more rain and the level was now higher, so consequently we stalled the quad and we had to float it out of the water. Not only did we stall it, as the cold water hit the hot motor, the steam burnt our legs.

There are lots of stories of what we kids used to get up to when we had 2000 acres to roam around on. Probably some things that Mum and Dad still don't know and it would be better if they never did.

Due to the number of accidents and how easily these can happen, I just want to re-iterate the safety of quadbikes needs to be taken seriously.

Quad bikes: Prepare safe, wear safe, ride safe

Many Australians have died or have been seriously injured from quad bikes (four-wheeled motorbikes) – including children.

Quad bikes are not ALL-terrain vehicles.

It's a popular belief that quad bikes can safely go on all kinds of terrain and surfaces. Unfortunately, this isn't true – riding on steep slopes, rough terrain and even hard, flat surfaces (such as tarmac and asphalt) may cause the quad bike to become unstable and very dangerous.

Quad bikes can be fun and useful to get around in, but can pose a number of safety hazards.

Even if you are an experienced rider, quad bikes can put you and your loved ones in danger

https://www.productsafety.gov.au/content/index.phtml/tag/quadbikes

What would you say are the 5 key elements for starting and running a successful business?

1. Be organised and keep detailed records
    Have a well organised filing cabinet. This can be either digital or a physical cabinet that stands in the corner. Just make sure it is logical and easily understood.
    Write down any procedures you use, so that as your business

grows and you have to get someone else to do various jobs, they know how you like each job to be completed.

By keeping detailed records, you'll know exactly where your business stands financially and what potential challenges you could be facing. Just knowing exactly where you are, gives you time to create strategies to overcome obstacles that can prevent you from being successful and growing your business.

2. Know your competition
    Don't be afraid of your competition, get to know them intimately. They may be doing something right that you can implement into your business and you both make more money.

3. Be creative and stay focused
    Always look for ways to improve your business, improve your systems and continually ask yourself, "Is there a better way to do this?"
    As you build your business, stay focused on achieving your short-term goals and never lose sight of your larger goals.

4. Be prepared to make sacrifices
    You think you are busy when making the decision to start your business but after you open your doors your work has just begun. In many cases, you will have to put more time and effort into your dream than you ever thought possible. You will have to make sacrifices, such as spending less time with family and friends, in order to be successful. This is where you need to stay focused on the reason why you are in business.

5. Provide a great service and be consistent
   If you provide a better service than your competitor and you are continually consistent with a high level of service and respect your customers will come to you the next time and the next and then next. Consistency is the key in making a successful business. You have to consistently keep doing the things necessary to be successful day in and day out.

Do you believe there is some sort of pattern or formula to becoming successful?

There are lots of formulas to becoming successful. However, they all pretty much say the same thing. My mentor

Decide what you WANT

PLAN on how you are going to get it

You, yourself take MASSIVE action

Change what you are DOING until you get what you want

The formula for success is:

Clarity

↓

Certainty

↓

Confidence

↓

Action

=

Success

Are your current actions getting you closer or further away from the outcome you want to achieve?

If you are running east looking for a sunset, it doesn't matter how committed you are. You won't get there. You have to make sure that what you're doing is leading you to where you really want to go.

> *"I want to do it because I want to do it. Women must try to do things as men have tried. When they fail, their failure must be but a challenge to others."*
>
> *Amelia Earhart*

Looking back, what's one thing you wish you understood about entrepreneurship before you ever got started?

Know what you do.
Do what you know.
Do what you love.
Businesses built around your strengths and talents will have a greater chance of success. If your heart isn't in it, you will not be successful.

If you could offer a first-time entrepreneur only one piece of advice, what would it be?

Being an entrepreneur doesn't mean you have to go it alone. Most successful business owners will tell you they could not have accomplished their goals without help - from a mentor, colleague or even your mum and dad.

No one knows everything, so don't come off as a know-it-all. Surround yourself with people who will nurture you to become a better leader and businesswoman. Find successful, knowledgeable individuals that share common interests and mutual business goals and who see value in working with you for the long-term.

What's the best business idea you have that you'll never use?

Not a business idea as such but more the process of accepting the fact that you wish to be in business. First comes the desire to own a business, then comes the process of deciding which business. It is a learning process that requires patience and persistence.

Inspiration:

If you could talk to one person from history, who would it be and why? Amelia Earhart.

Amelia Mary Earhart (Born July 24, 1897 – Disappeared July 2, 1937) was an American aviation pioneer and author.

Amelia Earhart was the first female aviator to fly solo across the Atlantic. She received the U.S. Distinguished Flying Cross for this record. She set many other records, wrote best-selling books about her flying experiences and was instrumental in the formation of The Ninety-Nines, an organisation for female pilots.

She joined the faculty of the Purdue University aviation department in 1935 as a visiting faculty member to counsel women on careers and help inspire others with her love of aviation. She was also a member of the National Woman's Party and an early supporter of the equal rights amendment.

During an attempt to make a circumnavigational flight of the globe in 1937, in a Purdue-funded Lockheed Model 10 Electra, Earhart disappeared over the central Pacific Ocean near Howland Island. Fascination with her life, career and disappearance continues to this day. http://www.ameliaearhart.com/about/bio2.html

What is your favourite book?

"Because a Little Bug Went Ka-Choo" by Dr Seuss.

This is a story of how little things can have a huge impact. When the little bug sneezes, he unknowing sets off a chain of events that wreaks havoc all across the countryside and eventually causes a catastrophe at the circus parade in town.

This book highlights the fact that for every action you perform there is a reaction, which causes another and so on. As the boys grew up they soon learnt that they got no sympathy with they tried something dumb. As my response to them would usually be a raise of the eyebrows "Well, the Little Bug went Ka-Choo" and they would just huff and puff then go about their merry way.

What do you want to be when you grow up?

When I grow up I want to be childlike again. By childlike I mean that I want to have no worries about where I am going to get the next feed from or where I am going to live.

I want to play with my husband and my kids, take them on holidays, go places, enjoy each other's company and play monopoly just because we can. Maybe they will all have wives and children but I would just like to enjoy them all.

I want to enjoy life and my lifestyle and enjoy my friends and acquaintances.

> *"When we are children we seldom think of the future. This innocence leaves us free to enjoy ourselves as few adults can. The day we fret about the future is the day we leave our childhood behind."*
>
> *Patrick Rothfuss, The Name of the Wind*

Where do you see yourself and your business in 10 or 20 years?

There have been a lot of lessons in my life over the last 20 years since having our own transport business but it doesn't matter what your age is, your stage in life or any disadvantages of shortcomings you may perceive, there is always a way for you to make a unique impact on the world and those around you.

That is why I want to help other women discover what sets them on fire and find a way to encourage them to achieve their goals and aspirations that will leverage who they are and make them come alive.

CHAPTER 7

Mary Koutalis

Optical Dispenser
To
Dump Truck Driver

Sydney
To
Western Australia

CHAPTER 7

Mary Koutalis
Optical Dispenser
To
Dump Truck Driver

Sydney
To
Western Australia

Mary Koutalis worked in the Optical Industry for 17 years throughout the eastern seaboard of Australia and got to a point of asking herself "Do I go to University and study for the next step up in Optometry for 5 years, or do I try something different?" She chose something different.

After looking at her options she decided to be a Mine Truck Driver and set about to get her HL license. She has shared with us some adventures of her life and the insights of changing her career and what she has discovered.

Why did you change what you wanted to do, Mary? What was the reason why you decided to go from optics into dump truck driving?

I started as an optical dispenser-in-training in 1985, straight out of school. I rang up to apply for a position and they said, "As a receptionist or a dispenser?" And I said, "Dispenser" but I had no idea what a dispenser was!

I went in for the interview and started a week and a half later as a trainee dispenser. That was in Sydney. I completed the dispensing course and obtained my diploma.

I worked with an optical retail chain all over metro Sydney for four years, and then I moved to Queensland. I had transferred with them, and I worked mostly in South East Queensland, but also in Townsville, the Sunshine Coast, the Gold Coast and out in Toowoomba. I had a ball. I was also fortunate enough to participate in Trachoma trips out in the Aboriginal settlements up in Murgon & Cherbourg, and out in Mungindi near Goondiwindi. An amazing experience! I lived in Qld for seven years, then I thought, okay... time for a life change. I was at a point where things were getting a bit stale and I was hungry to learn something new.

A rep for an optical wholesale lens manufacturing came into work and I was talking to him. They were a manufacturer of lenses and semi-finished lens blanks down in South Australia. They supplied surfacing laboratories with lenses and blanks so they could grind the prescription into the lenses, and supplied them to retail optical outlets. They had a job position available down in Sydney, so I applied and later secured the position. I stayed with them for 17 great years.

We were wholesalers. The new position entailed visiting those retail outlets and promoting our products. We were dependent on the laboratories to do the right thing; when an optometrist said that he wanted to order our lenses, we had to hope that the laboratory wouldn't substitute our lenses with another brand of lens and supply them instead.

There was a big change in the market at that time. One of our competitors bought a laboratory group that used to be one of our biggest customers and that was the start of polarisation in the wholesale optical industry. There are very fewer independent practices left, which is really sad because small business is the backbone of the country. No matter what business you look at, it is happening. The big guys are gobbling up the smaller guys. Everything, everywhere you turn.

In the seventeen years I've worked in Melbourne, Queensland, New South Wales and also Western Australia.

> *"When one door of happiness closes, another opens but often we look so long at the closed door that we do not see the one which has been opened for us."*
>
> *Helen Keller*

So, "What's next?!" The next step in optics would be for me to university and study optometry full time for 5 years and then at the end of 5 years, where do I work? I'd probably end up working for a large retail chain. For me personally, I just needed something new to learn. I was at that point where I needed to try something different.

So I thought, Okay, education-wise, what areas am I gifted in? What can I transfer across? What are my interests?

I do have an interest in workplace safety. I'm now living in WA, and what are the main industries that apply a strong priority and focus to workplace safety in WA? The mining industry of course.

So, I get some education to get some work in the mines. Even if I can't get work in the mines, if I can get an education in work health and safety I can transfer that into a new and different industry and it'll open up a lot more doors.

My initial intention was to secure an entry level position by becoming a truck driver. "Go and drive trucks in the mines because everyone's talking about driving trucks in the mines." So I thought yep, okay, as a base entry, that's probably the most direct way to get a foot in the door. Not quite... as I found out! The mining industry has undergone some major changes as well. The prices of iron ore and coal has taken a hit resulting in a lot of businesses diversifying, cutting back on staff, shelving projects, or even shutting down. For some companies, it was no longer sustainable. This has resulted in a rather large pool of experienced workers for the mining industry employers to choose from at the present. So now, all the adverts say a minimum of two to three years' experience.

So I needed to take a different path. I had done a lot of driving over the years and a lot of country driving and loved that so I thought, "Okay well, that's one element that I'm fine with" because obviously if I don't like driving there's no point in applying for a job where I'm driving a truck.

So, the first step was to take some lessons and obtain my open HR (heavy rigid) drivers' license. I loved it! Here I was, swapping my suits and high heels for some steel capped boots and big wheels. Now I am licensed to drive a road ranger truck. I almost couldn't believe it. So far so good. Then I took the next step, and did another course. This time, it was to obtain my haul truck ticket. I passed that too, and I'm really enjoying driving these big trucks. Loved it even more than I thought I would. Okay, there's another box ticked, I like this, this is a good thing. Right! I can do this!

My plan was to get an entry-level position in the mines driving a truck. If I can do that for a couple of years and if I like it, great, I can continue with that. In the meantime, I can then obtain my work health and safety qualifications. I know I have to start at the ground and work up, but that is exciting too. If I want to perform a safety role I really need to know the job. I want to learn the job from the ground up so I can be a good safety officer, and not someone that just comes in and doesn't have an idea of what the job entails. If I want to progress and create a career path for myself in the work health and safety area, hopefully, I can then become a health and safety representative. Later on I can then progress further to become a health safety committee member, and then advisor. So there's a career path there, if I want to.

Alternatively, the other option is to start as a truck driver and then become an all-rounder and get trained on some of the other machines such as dozers, graders, loaders, excavators etc. The hours are long and you're away from home a lot, but I'm used to that anyway. Well, making the decision is the hardest part. Once you've made the decision, everything else just starts to fall into place a little bit.

What would have been some of your failures and what did you learn from them?

In my last job, well, we all did, as a team. We all did a lot of extra hours, a lot of extra work. There was no extra pay but we wanted to do it. We wanted to be the best that we could be, and we just rolled our sleeves up and got on with it, and loved it. We were like a family. We still keep in touch. But in the more recent years, management made the decision to move our manufacturing off-shore and re-locate it to some of our other sister sites overseas, which was more cost-effective. Our competitors had been doing it for years and we held back, because we were Australian-based originally. With it all going off-shore, it felt like a different company. When that started happen, I just felt like a massive big part of me went with that. When I looked back, everything that we'd worked for, it was like, "Well what was it for, because it's all gone! I remember when that company had over 1,200 people employed in the prescription lens division in Australia when I started. It was thriving! When I left in late 2013, I think it was down to less than 30 people.

As a result, I don't think that I managed my work-life balance very well. I was so driven on the job that my private life suffered as a result. In hindsight, it was still just a job. That was a decision I had made at the time, so I take full accountability for that, but in the future, a job is a job and, your life is your life, and as a friend of mine said, "Nobody's ever died wishing they'd have worked more."

But you know, I have no regrets. In future, I would definitely manage work and my personal life in a better way

What sort of thing were you most satisfied with, looking back?

There have been quite a few things. I love travel so about 4½ years ago I flew to Perth and did a trip across Australia on my own. I took four to 5 weeks. It was awesome doing it on my own. I met people from all walks of life who had different stories and I spent New Year's Eve on a cattle farm.

I met this old couple at Balladonnia and they lived at Port Lincoln, and they said, "Oh, when you come to Port Lincoln, you must come visit us!" And so I did, I went and visited them at Port Lincoln. We're still in touch.

> *"Make your purpose more than just making money.*
> *Make it inspiring."*
>
> **Kim Kiyosaki**

I did a lot of random things, like a shark cage dive where they feed the sharks and swimming with wild sea lions. I saw some amazing scenery. It was so incredibly invigorating and liberating. I didn't have anything booked. I could stop wherever I wanted to, whenever I wanted to and I slept in just about every day.

I did a 5 day cattle drive on horseback in the Victorian high. You had your own group of cattle to herd along, and we were all sitting around a campfire at night, swapping stories over a few drinks and sleeping in swags.

I did a trip around the south island of New Zealand in a camper, climbed a glacier went ski-dooing and snow skiing amongst other things. I took a trip to Thailand where we did a trek up in Northern Chaing Mai. We stayed up in the hillside villages and arrived there by riding elephants and climbing up the rice paddies. It was amazing and very grounding.

Who inspires you?

You're going to laugh at this one. I used to be inspired by the poem, The Man from Snowy River. I had a horse in my late teens, a quarter horse, who was my world and I loved that horse to death.

People inspire me. Everyone has a different story. I love listening to these stories, and learning from other people's experiences. Words of wisdom.

What do you want to do? Where do you want to go? Where do you see yourself in the next 10 to 20 years?

In the next 10 years, I'll complete my traineeship and obtain my Cert III in Surface Extraction. I'll also complete my Diploma in Work Health and Safety. Both of those qualifications have extended levels where further study can produce a higher qualification. This is something I'll consider when the time comes. I'd also like to do a few more courses down the track. By then, my current role will have developed further, and I'll have a better idea of where this new career path will take me.

Currently, I'm driving 300 tonne haul trucks and loving it. My wonderful partner and I are on the same roster and on the same mine-site so we can see each other frequently. This creates a fantastic work-life balance. In our off-weeks we can relax, socialize, travel or go interstate to visit our families.

Up north in the mines, we work long hours but we're getting paid for it. It's a whole different culture, it's a different way of learning things that in itself is great. It's not easy. There are elements that are tough, and being green I'm making a few mistakes, but that is a part of learning something new. I'm starting at the very, very bottom, and working my way up, in a male-dominated industry. I have no delusions about it, but you know what, I'm up for it.

What do you see as some of your challenges?

Learning the job is my current challenge.

Getting the feeling of the size and the spacial perception of the truck body. The truck weighs 300 tonnes. To drive a vehicle of this size is incredible and really fun! Learning to drive a left hand drive vehicle in an off road environment in all weather conditions. Learning and observing Priority rules which are different to regular road rules when on site. Learning the truck components - in the cabin, externally, and yes I also have to climb underneath. Getting used to the long nearly 14 hour shifts - days and nights. Working on public holidays and missing special events like Christmas with your family. Getting used to the way of FIFO life. I'm used to regular travel and long hours, but there would be many where this lifestyle would not be suitable. Getting used to camp food. Getting used to the politics. It's a whole new world.

Starting a new career at the age of 47 is challenging but so invigorating. It's fantastic to be learning something new. This is in addition to my studies.

The people we have on our site are all come from different walks of life, and they all have a story. Some of these stories are absolutely amazing. I have found everyone is willing to help and provide guidance and assistance to the less experienced operators. It's a very respectful working environment. Much better than I could ever have expected.
I have gone from "high heels to big wheels". I've had an amazing career change, going into an environment where steel toe boots, hard hats and

High Vis work wear are the norm. Going from a clean, medical based profession to an industry where we work with dirt, diesel and dust! And loving it!

I have a direction and a plan. Making the decision is the hard part. You've just got to start somewhere. Make a decision, create a plan, work the plan, and then flesh it out from there. You never know where it might take you.

"If you face your fears head on you will succeed and in turn you will become almost fearless."

Marilyn Wood

CHAPTER 8

Marilyn Wood

Engineer

Western Australia

CHAPTER 8

Marilyn Wood
Engineer
Western Australia

Bachelor of Engineering in Civil Engineering from Sydney University - BEng Syd
Master of Engineering (Honours) from Wollongong University - MEng (Hons) Woll
Bachelor of Laws from Queensland University of Technology - BLaw QUT

Marilyn Wood is a Civil Engineer from WA and is an amazing woman who was the 2nd female to graduate from the University of NSW with an engineering degree in the 1970's. She has since furthered her education with another Engineering degree and a Law degree whilst bringing up her 3 sons. Through her career she has worked in many unusual places from Norilsk in Russia and New Caledonia in the Pacific Ocean.

She is a true inspiration and is the Author of "The Odd One Out" which is about her life and how she dealt with life's challenges to benefit others who have chosen careers where they are the odd one out.

What ignited the spark and passion for engineering and why did you choose this career?

I am a civil engineer and have been working in engineering, specifically in the mining engineering industry, for my entire working career. My main reason for choosing this career was to make sure that I could always support myself and be independent. I did not want to be subservient to or dependent on anyone else. My father was a really domineering person and I could see that if my mother had been able to support herself she would have had options. I also wanted to do something meaningful with my life. I did well at school and wanted to make the most of my gifts.

Is it what you expected?

Mostly my career has been as I expected it would be. My career has provided well for me and my family financially. I have also felt extremely fulfilled and privileged to have been able to achieve the things I have in engineering. There were times that caused me pain. I have been very isolated a lot of the time as I have been the only female and definitely the odd one out. It has also been a little difficult to juggle home life and work at times. Engineering is not a part time job, especially the work I have done which has been working in the mining industry in Australia and overseas.

If you had the chance to start your career over again, knowing what you now know, what would you do differently?

I would probably go down exactly the same path as I have done. I may make different choices in relation to marriage and my work/life balance but I would still have children and challenge myself the way I have done.

What 3 pieces of advice would you give to women who want to embark on a career that is in a male dominated industry?

1. You (and only you) are in charge of your destiny – that is you determine what you want to do, how you want to be perceived and how far you want to go in whatever field you are in. You

cannot blame anyone else for your failures (or your successes). It is up to you.

2.   Your world is a reflection of you so if you are unhappy, the world around you will be unhappy. It is up to you to be positive so your world around you will also be positive. Treat yourself seriously and with respect and others, even your male colleagues, will do the same.

3.   The same challenges will come to you until you figure out what lesson you are supposed to be getting from the challenge. Figure out what is happening to you and why, learn the lesson and move on.

What are your ideals towards life?

It's probably summed up in my advice but basically your life is in your hands, no one else's. Your life is a gift from the universe (or God or whoever you believe in). What you make of yourself is your gift to the universe or whoever you believe in so it is up to you to make the absolute most of the opportunities that you are given in every aspect of your life.

How do you define success?

I define success as:

- Myself and my family being fit and healthy
- Being able to provide well for my family now and in the future, both financially and in moral support
- To feel fulfilled and have a sense of achievement
- To feel as though I have made a contribution

What have been some of your failures and what have you learned from them?

Unfortunately, earlier in my life I did not have the same balance as I do now. This has meant that I do not have a partner. This is compensated for now by being very close to my sons and their families. I do now have a good balance of work and relaxation in my life and I truly enjoy my freedom and independence.

> *"Never tell a young person that something cannot be done. God may have been waiting centuries for someone ignorant enough of the impossible to do that very thing."*
>
> *G. M. Trevelyan*

What is your greatest fear and how do you manage fear?

I really do not have any fears but if I had to say something it would be the thought that the security, health and safety of me or my family is threatened. My way of dealing with this thought is to remind myself of the fact that my world is a reflection of me and I am in control of my destiny. That is why I choose to see and have good things in my life.

Some of the situations I have experienced have been truly daunting to begin with but if you face your fears head on you will succeed and in turn you will become almost fearless.

What do you consider to be your greatest achievement and what's the single most important reason for your success thus far?

I have a number of great achievements.

From a personal point of view, I have three beautiful sons who are now three magnificent caring men.

In my engineering career I have reached the highest level of achievement. That is, being the project manager of large projects which have been delivered on time and on budget and all those associated with the projects were happy to have those associations.

I have significant educational qualifications. I love to learn and will continue to do so until I leave this life.

In my other interests, I have managed to acquire significant assets which will support me independently for the rest of my life.

> *"Few things in the world are more powerful than a positive push. A smile, a world of optimism and hope and a "you can do it" when things are tough."*
>
> **Richard M Devos**

My most recent success will be the publishing of my first book which is mainly about my life and how I have dealt with life's challenges. Hopefully this will benefit others who have chosen careers or situations where they are the odd one out, as I have been.

The reason I have achieved success so far has a lot to do with being determined to succeed and putting in the effort required to do this. I have always kept the end goals in my mind.

Earlier in my career it was not as easy as it is now because I was very much "the odd one out" and my activities were highly scrutinised so I had to do well or much better than my cohorts. My father said to me when I graduated, "People will be looking for your failures much more than they will notice your successes." I have always been aware of this and it has helped me a lot. I aim not to do anything I would regret in the future. The song "No Regrets" by Edith Piaf sums this up.

How has this change in career affected your family life?

I will answer this question as a comparison to what is considered a "normal career for a female." The fact that I have been an engineer is probably not as significant as the fact that I chose to be a project manager of mining engineering projects which has necessitated me spending significant time away from my family.

Being away from my family was really tough for me and, at times, for my sons when they were growing up. However, when I was at home I devoted my whole time to looking after my family especially being with them and cooking for them. In some respects this separation built an independence into my sons which has benefited them in their lives.

As I have said previously, the fact that I put a lot of effort into my career probably did not do my marriage any good. This may have ended anyway because I continued to grow whereas my partner hated change.

What is the strangest thing you've ever done or seen on this journey?

Wow! That is a big question. I have had some strange and amazing things happen. I have been to many unusual places with my work, from Norilsk in Russia to New Caledonia in the Pacific Ocean. Because a number of the projects I have worked on have been such that there would be significant impact on the local community, I have had to put myself in their shoes and really get to know whatever community I was in. I visited these places when they were places people just did not go to. This has been very challenging at times but overall truly rewarding. It has taught me that we are all very similar, aiming to protect and provide for our families. Genuine regard for your and other people's wellbeing is the most important thing to have.

What would you say are the 5 key elements for being a successful engineer?

My 5 key elements for being successful are to:

1. Have integrity in everything you do
2. Make sure you are educated in whatever you try to do, either in formal education or experience. I have 2 engineering degrees and a law degree.
3. Build a rapport with the people you are dealing with and put yourself in their shoes
4. Remember you have to be what you want to see in people you deal with
5. Persevere and put in the effort required; do not give up, that is

the easy path

What organisations and businesses have been instrumental in your career?

Generally, I believe that you make your own opportunities.

However, there have been individuals in all of the companies I have worked for who have put their trust in me to do a good job and I am very grateful to all of these people. It did help to get the right qualifications and experience and to be prepared to do any job no matter how menial or challenging so long as it was useful in the long term.

What has been your most satisfying moment?

I have had many satisfying moments; it is hard to choose just one. Amongst the most satisfying moments I would include:

- When I graduated from Sydney University with my engineering degree
- The births of each of my three sons
- Having the money to personally buy and live in a house on the beach in Western Australia
- Leaving full time work to devote myself to what I want to do

Looking back, what's one thing you wish you'd understood about the industry before you ever got started?

It is really all up to you and what you are prepared to do.

If you could offer only one piece of advice to a first-time female looking at getting involved in this industry, what would it be?

Make sure you are committed to this career, it is not something you can half do. There will be great rewards but there will also be many difficult times which you need to have a lot of strength and perseverance to survive. It is not for the faint hearted.

> *"It's very important for women entering into the industry to be authentic to themselves, deliver results to the business and be recognised that way and not feel any pressure to change the person that they are."*
>
> *Julie Shuttleworth*

If you could talk to one person from history, who would it be and why?

This is not something I really think too much about. I can empathise with a number of people but I do think that your life's journey is your own so I have aimed to make my own life truly inspiring, to have absolutely no regrets in any area of my life and to make the most of every moment.

Who has been your greatest inspiration?

My greatest inspiration has been my sons and the desire to be the best mother and provider for them.

Do you have a favourite book?

I have many favourite books, both fiction and non-fiction. I love to read and see how other people view the world and deal with life.

A book that made a great impression early on was "The Power of One" by Bryce Courtenay. There is a paragraph which talks about a young sapling struggling to survive but is being choked by vines growing all over it. If the sapling remains strong and persists it will survive and grow to be tall and strong.

At the time I read this I was having career and personal issues – this helped. I have thought about this many times over the years.

How do you go about marketing yourself for any prospective employment roles?

Find out everything about the position you are applying for and tailor your CV to highlight the experience you have had to bring to this role. In engineering, education and experience is the most important thing. If you have appropriate experience you will exude confidence and that will get you the job. Act with integrity and it will pay off.

What do you want to be when you grow up?

I would like to acquire more property and to do more property developing, mainly with my own property portfolio. I want to use all of my educational and organisational skills to benefit me and my family more directly. I would also like to become a successful author and, through my books, help others in their life's journey.

Where you see yourself in 10 years or 20 years?

I see myself continuing along the same path of engineering consulting and also using these skills in property development. I would like to help others via my books.

I travel a lot and will continue to do so for extended periods so that I can really get to know the communities I travel to.

On a personal level, I will be spending as much quality time as possible with my family and helping them wherever possible.

CHAPTER 9

Julie Shuttleworth

General Manager
Fortescue's Solomon Mine

CHAPTER 9

Julie Shuttleworth
General Manager
Fortescue's Solomon Mine

Western Australia
2014 Excellence in Mining Award,
2014 Murdoch Distinguished Alumni Award
2013 CME Women in Resource Champion
2012 WA Business Woman of the Year
2011 Australian Mining Mine Manager of the Year
2013 WIM (UK) 100 Global Inspiration Women in Mining
2014 Australian Financial Review Westpac 100 Women of Influence

Julie Shuttleworth graduated from Murdoch University with a double major in Extractive Metallurgy and Chemistry and has more than 20 years' experience in the mining industry in Australia, China and Tanzania. Her career has progressed from Plant Metallurgist, Senior Metallurgist, Process Superintendent, and Process Manager to General Manager Positions. Julie has held General Manager Positions at Barrick's Buzwagi Mine in Tanzania, Barrick's Granny Smith Mine in WA, Fortescue's Cloudbreak Mine in WA, and is currently General Manager at Fortescue's Solomon Mine.

Julie has a strong focus on safety leadership, teamwork and positive attitude. Julie mentors many mining professionals, and regularly speaks at universities, schools, conferences and seminars. She also sponsors the Julie Shuttleworth Prize in Mineral Processing at Murdoch University.

The outdoors lifestyle calls her when she has time off and Julie enjoys scuba diving, surfing, rock climbing, canyoning, hiking, underwater photography and has travelled to over 100 countries.

You were the General Manager of Fortescue Cloudbreak Mine in Western Australia, clearly you have a passion for mining. What ignited the spark for the love of what you do?

It started off with my love of science in high school, particularly chemistry and I also liked rocks, geology and big machinery. I liked outback places and I didn't want to just work in a lab inside all day in my white lab coat! I wanted a job which combined chemistry with rocks, geology, big machines and trucks and which gave me an opportunity to travel.

I decided to study a double major in Chemistry and Extractive Metallurgy (Mineral Science). The end result of this study was to become a metallurgist. During my university holidays I did vacation work at several mine sites. As a vacation student you get to do lots of manual labour around the process plants, work which no one else really wants to do! I worked hard to prove I could do the job just as good as anyone else. This included hosing slurry, shovelling piles of material that had built up by conveyors, unbogging crushers and chutes, picking steel pipes out of ore before it went to the crushers and pulverising samples in the laboratory.

Vacation work was a fantastic way to get hands on experience in the industry and to work out if I would like it or not. I just loved it; working in the outback, the different people you get to work with in the team, and learning about different technologies, equipment and processes to produce a final metal product. It was great! It gets in your blood, that's for sure. I realised this is what I wanted to do and it confirmed my career choice to be a metallurgist.

How would you define success?

For me, being successful is being happy and satisfied at what you do. Also success is setting your goals and achieving them or at least being happy with the outcomes of your efforts.

What would be your most satisfying moment in your career?

For me a career highlight was when I was involved with the Buzwagi Project in Tanzania in 2006 to 2009. I was involved with doing the feasibility study and bringing that project from the paper, through design engineering, procurement of the equipment, organising contract services, construction, recruiting and training a team, commissioning the process plant to make the first gold bars and taking it into operation. A great achievement was that over 90% if our Tanzanian employees had never worked in mining before so we created lots of jobs too.

That whole process of bringing a mine from paper through to the actual operation was a fantastic highlight. It was the first time I'd ever done that. Then I became General Manager of that mine shortly afterwards at the age of 35, which was another great achievement.

How have your motivations changed since you first left university?

I don't think that my motivations have actually changed. I've always been positive and I've always been driven, set my goals and achieved them. I have a positive outlook and just work through any challenges that come up.

Since leaving university I certainly have a broader view now and am not so narrow minded, and this is a result of working and traveling overseas. I have also learnt to be more patient!

I was also such a scrooge when I left university, saving and investing everything, being very tight with my money to the point I didn't treat myself with many things. Having progressed my career and being financially comfortable now, I find it easier to spend on myself, such as travelling and recreational fun things, but $20 is still a lot of money for me and I'm sure not going to waste it.

With your high responsibility job, how do you get good life balance?

I really enjoy the fly-in/fly-out (FIFO) lifestyle. When I worked overseas I was on rosters such as 60 days on and 20 days off, or nine weeks on and four weeks off. During that time off I'd go travelling around the world and do all the fun things I like to do such as hiking, canyoning and scuba diving.

Since 2010 I've been back working in Australia and I've been on shorter rosters such as eight days on and six days of, or four days on and three days off. When I have six days off, or even just three days, I've got something planned, either a short trip overseas or somewhere in Australia, to go hiking or scuba diving. I've travelled to over 100 countries, so yes I definitely have the travel bug!

It's important I keep doing those things that I really like to do as it charges me up and gives me positive energy, which keeps me positive at work as well. I've noticed that when I go for a long period without doing any travel, I actually start feeling a little bit down and need re-charging.

For me life is not all just about work, but having fun and being happy. When I'm 85 or 90 in a rocking chair on my verandah I want to be happy with everything I've done.

I encourage everyone to make the time to do the things that recharge you and give you positive energy. You have to make it happen for yourself. Make the time to do it, and don't make excuses!

How has being a FIFO worker affected your family life?

My partner's great, we've been together for 15 years after meeting in Africa. He is also from Western Australia, and enjoys traveling, hiking, scuba diving and other outdoors activities as well. We were lucky to be working at the same mine site, on the same roster, so we did a lot of travelling together on our days off.

When we moved back to Australia he was at another mine site on the same roster as me, so we could still spend time together on our days off. He then started working out of the corporate office and now runs his own business from home, this suits me perfectly as now I'm on a four days on, three days off roster so I see him every weekend. It works out well.

FIFO really works for us. It's great working at the mine, I can work the long hours to get work done during the week and then when at home we can have quality time together, go on short trips to have fun outdoors or visit family and friends. FIFO is actually less stressful for me than a city job. For us right now, it actually works perfectly.

What would a day in the life of Julie Shuttleworth be like? What would that consist of?

As General Manager of a mine, I am responsible for everything that happens on the mine site. In particular the safety of everyone that works at the site, and ensuring compliance to legislation including the Mines Safety & Inspection Act and Regulations and environmental requirements. My team is responsible for meeting the safety, production and cost targets of the mine. At Solomon Mine, I am responsible for over 2000 people, production of 70 million tonnes of iron ore per year and a budget of over $1 billion per year.

A normal workday consists of getting up at around 4:15 am, getting some breakfast at 'the mess', packing my lunch and going to the mine site. It's about a 20 minute drive to the mine from camp.

At around 5:30am I go to a pre-start meeting somewhere around the mine site, for example in the maintenance workshop, out in the mining hub or in the process plant, where the teams talk about safety and what they're going to be doing for the day.

Then I'll spend several hours out in the field, seeing what's going on, talking with people on the job, particularly about safety but this also makes me available for any questions that they have. This is really important to me because it shows the team that I'm approachable and that makes them comfortable coming to me if they've got issues and I also learn more about what they're doing. It's very important for me that leaders spend time in the field, and I like to lead by example.

Some examples of field instructions include sitting in a truck or excavator with the equipment operator, walking around the ore processing facility with process operators, going to the maintenance workshop and talking to the fitters, or talking to anyone on the mine site in their workplace. We've got over two thousand people working at the mine, there so there's a range different people I can go and speak to, and I get to a different area every day.

The rest of the day is filled with conference calls, meetings, presentation, planning, forecasting, strategising, making decisions, approving various items including expenditures and mine plans, and helping people with any issues they have. It's my job to make sure everything is in place for safe, cost effective, efficient production, so I need to keep decisions moving. A daily focus for me is safety leadership. I also track production results and any challenges to make sure that we're optimising the business.

I leave the office at 6pm, have dinner, try to do some exercise, maybe catch up on any outstanding work matters (or preferably organise my next holiday), then aim to get 6 to 7 hours sleep.

Every day is completely different and I have to be flexible depending on the priority at the time - but every day is always full and flies by.

What is the strangest thing that you've ever done?

One of the strangest things that I've ever done was when I was working in China. To my knowledge, this was the first time that a western company had operated a gold mine in China. I had to take two gold bars that weighed 15kg each to the bank to sell them.

We were escorted by the police for several hours through the mountains to the bank in the nearest city, with the gold bars sitting beside me in a box.

I went into the bank and handed the gold bars over to the bank manager to weigh, but we struck a problem. Our bars weighed 15kg and the bank scales only weighed up to 5 kilograms. That's when we realised all the other gold mines in China only make small gold bars.

I thought "Crikey, what am I going to do? I can't go back to the mine without the money and I can't go to another bank." The mine had lots of bills to pay, including the workers, so I had to find a solution!

So I asked the Chinese driver to go up the street to the hardware store to get a hacksaw and some hacksaw blades! The bank manager pulled out a table and there we were sitting in the bank, in the middle of China hacksawing these two gold bars into thirds with a hacksaw! Gold filings were flying everywhere and people were walking in and out of the bank like it happens every day. Of course, it doesn't happen every day, and it's probably never happened to anyone else in the world, but finally we had those gold bars chopped into thirds and did the transaction. The mine got the money, the bank got the gold, and everyone was happy! Obviously we don't sell gold bars like that in Australia!

In case you're wondering, I did sweep up all the gold filings and took them back to the mine to put in with next gold pour.

There are quite a few interesting and strange experiences that happened whilst in China. It was a really interesting place to work back then in the late '90s.

What are some other challenges you've had and how have you overcome them?

I don't really sit around and think about the challenges that I've had throughout my career and when people ask me that, it takes me a while to think of them. They're not really major ones. I think I've been really lucky with my positive attitude and high level of confidence. I tend to work right through them without even thinking too much about them as challenges.

One of the hardest things were when I was working overseas for 12 years on longer rosters. I really missed by family and friends back in Australia, especially mum and dad. There were a lot of things that I couldn't do, such as my friends weddings, and I missed my grandmother's funeral as I couldn't get there on time. I'm really close my family and I really did miss them. That was one of the hardest things.

One example from early in my career as a Graduate Metallurgist, I was put in charge of running the metallurgical laboratory. There was one particular metallurgical technician who reported to me, who'd completed his university degree in metallurgy except for one unit, and had ten years' experience. He liked to prove that he knew everything and that I knew nothing and he really wanted to prove it to everybody. This was tough as I had just come out of university with minimal experience and had to be his supervisor, but I worked through it and it was probably one of my first lessons in leadership.

Working in China a key challenge was communication. I had an interpreter by my side for a lot of the working day, however he didn't always translate what I wanted, especially when I had to have difficult discussions and discipline people he would get off track. Another example is that one evening I asked the night shift fitter to put a guard on the pump to improve safety, as the pulleys were exposed. When I came back the next morning, I could see the job wasn't done, so asked about the guard. The response was "Yes Miss Julie, the guard has been standing there all night". They had organised for a person to stand next to the pump to guard it, rather than put the guard over the pulley!. So those experiences taught me the importance of making sure people understand what you communicate and not just assume they've understood.

Working in Tanzania, there are not many women that work in the mining industry, especially higher professional or manager jobs. I got promoted to be Process Manager by the age of 30, responsible for approximately 350 people. People often ask if this was challenging as the general culture in Tanzania is to respect older men, and it was unusual for a young woman to be the manager. I didn't really find this any issue at all, and I think this was because over several years I had built up respectful relationships with the team members. I had gone over there to train Tanzanians who were working in the processing plant as a metallurgists, operators and maintenance personnel. They had worked with me on the tools, in the plant, getting covered with slurry, and they knew I had worked with them and trained them, so that built up respect for when I went into that first Manager role. An important part was that I was also approachable, and that I had delivered many successful metallurgical projects for the business.

At the age of 35 I was promoted to General Manager which was a challenge as now I was responsible for the whole mine site, it wasn't just in the processing plant any more, which is where I was very comfortable after 15 years' experience in plants.

Moving into the General Manager role I was responsible for safety of the whole mine site, community and government relations, environment, the large mining team, mobile maintenance, geology, warehouse and supply chain; all those things that I'd never been fully responsible for before.

In particular, working in Africa, there are a lot of other things you've got to deal with. For example you've got the interaction with government officials and community leaders on a very regular basis as well as potential thefts from the mine site because of poverty in the area. You've got to train up a workforce that has not worked in mining before and operate to western standards at the same time. I received many phone calls throughout the night and there was always a lot to deal with. That year as General Manger in Tanzania was the toughest and most stressful job I've had to date, but I sure learnt a lot.

One of the other challenges was that I had to go to meetings with the local government officials and they ignored me most of the time. It was just their culture not to take much notice of a young woman so I didn't take it to heart, I still showed respect and remained authentic to myself and represented the company correctly. The previous General Manager was an older male and he had found it much easier than I did in this area.

One great thing though was that as a company we were able to build many schools in the local area. I represented the company at the official opening of one of these schools. After my speech, the President of Tanzania did his speech, and called me back to the stage to stand with him and use me as an example to all the women that they could do great things, and how great it was that I was a woman managing the mine. That was a great experience, and after that all the government officials that had ignored me before became quite friendly.

An interesting career change was coming back to Western Australia after having worked overseas for 12 years. I was General Manager of an underground mine and I had never managed an underground mine before, and I had never been in a management position in Australia. There was also uncertainty from many of the underground miners about having a female General Manager, which they'd never had before. I overcame this by spending a lot of time in the field with various team members, learning what they did and showing them I was approachable and focused on safety. As a General Manager you do not need to know every detail, instead delegate and empower people to do their jobs. I stayed authentic to myself and my leadership style and I had a very successful three years in that position.

Another career change was when, after 20 years in gold mining, I took on the role of General Manager of Cloudbreak Mine, a large iron ore mine, having never worked in iron ore before.

The main things about working through any challenges, is to have confidence in yourself, be authentic, have a positive outlook, and go for it! Never worry that you don't have all the perfect experience, you will learn that as you go. If you are given opportunities outside your comfort zone, I encourage you to 'go for it!'

Did you ever feel that your safety was at risk in any of those situations in any country?

No, I never felt my safety was at risk. Safety was a high priority for the companies I worked for. Due to the poverty in the area there was always the risk and events of theft. You have to be aware and not put yourself at risk in any way.

How do you go about finding people to bring into your team that truly care about the project the way you do?

To me, when I have to recruit someone into the team I firstly make sure that they've got an unwavering safety commitment; the safety of their team is a key focus, that they lead by example and set the highest safety standards and accountability. That's the most important thing. It's also important that they've got a very positive attitude are self-motivated and obviously they've got to demonstrate technical know-how and leadership that has delivered results previously in any area that I'm recruiting them for.

When I recruit, the positions I'm generally looking for are department managers who have to manage from 100 to 1000 people (depending on the area of responsibility). That takes a very competent person, and I'm looking for someone who has that energy about them.

You've got to have energy to really make a difference and you've got to also be in tune with what's going on. In summary, I look for someone who's got an unwavering standard for safety and positive attitude who is approachable and authentic with all the required experience for the role.

If you had the chance to start your career over again, what would you do differently?

I'd probably try and stress less, particularly in the first 16 years of my career. I definitely have a better handle on managing stress now. Having said that, I went to a stress management course several years ago and I realised that I don't have much to worry about because everyone else seemed much more stressed than I did.

Something I think about now is; will it really matter in 2 days' time, or 2 weeks' time, or in 20 years' time? That helps put it in perspective and helps reduce stress of the moment.

I just like to be a perfectionist which puts self-induced pressure or stress on yourself, unnecessarily. I could have learnt earlier not to try to do everyone else's job. Don't try to do everything for everyone else because you want it done quickly or to the standards you want. It will cause late nights as you work longer hours trying to get it all done and means you leave less time for you. It takes a little bit longer sometimes but you've got to let people do the job for themselves, you can't do everything. I had to learn to be more patient and wait a bit longer for things to be done, but it was much better once I learnt this, and now I am very good at delegating!

What three pieces of information would you give college students who want to get involved in the mining industry?

Firstly you've got to understand the different career opportunities that are out there and choose one that really interests you so that you are doing something you enjoy. Not many people get the opportunity to get out on a mine whilst at school to take a closer look, but there are other ways you can find out. For example: attend industry career days, research careers on the internet, and go to universities or other educational facilities to find out more about the mining related courses they offer. Obviously an important step is to make sure you're doing the subjects at high school that will get you into what you want to do.

I was lucky enough to go to a Science Summer School at Murdoch University during high school holidays which gave me a great insight into various science careers and courses. I also visited several universities and read their prospectuses to learn more about their courses, and I read the careers book provided by my school from cover to cover. You need to be proactive when it comes to your career decisions.

Secondly, if you're at university, aim to get vacation work at the mines during your summer holidays to make sure you like it. For me this was key in giving me an early understanding of what the mining industry was about. It made me realise 'Yeah, I really love this. I want to keep doing it.' Understanding that early on is good.

For example, one of the girls doing the metallurgy course with me went to a mine on a field trip and realised she was scared of heights and found it really difficult walking up the stairs. Being a metallurgist and not being able to go up heights is a bit of an issue because that's what you'll be doing every day if you work on process plants.

Thirdly, once you start studying a mining related course, I encourage you to get involved with networking. Join an industry body such as the Australian Institute of Mining and Metallurgy (AusIMM), attend their functions and meet other people already working in the industry. Establishing these relationships often helps you land your first job!

What would you say would be the five key elements to starting and running a successful project?

The five key elements:-

- Have a positive attitude

- Be authentic to yourself

- Be confident

- Be practical

- Set your goals

Communicate what your true aspirations are to other people who can help you along the way and ask for help when you need it.

It's key to deliver results for the business. For women in the industry, we cannot sit around thinking things should be different because of our gender. You've just got to get on with it. Deliver results for the business. Lead by example. Have confidence in yourself and deliver results that make the senior management recognise you. That's what earns you recognition, promotions and respect along the way.

A lot of it comes down to being confident in yourself. That's something we all have to continue to work on, as well as learning how to communicate and present yourself well.

The other important thing is to get a good lifestyle balance, smile, have fun and enjoy life.

Is there one thing you wish you'd understood about management before you got into the role of management?

I learned about leadership and management along the way and step by step I got there. Something that's important to learn is that you can't keep everybody happy with every decision you make. You've got to learn to accept that and not stress or worry about trying to keep everybody happy with every decision. Also it's important to realise that you can't do everything yourself. You have to learn to delegate and empower others.

Looking back early in my career, I sometimes lacked confidence to speak up and say what I thought. I'd hang back a bit and not sit at the main meeting table. One of my mentors encouraged to "sit at the table and say what you think". It really encouraged me to be more present and contribute. I think it's important to have someone to help mentor you along the way. I also remember I used to come to work with my shirt hanging out. When I became a superintendent, I started tucking it in. That was a small thing but I realised that I needed to look more professional in that role.

If you could talk to one person from history, who would it be and why?

I like those scientists from the 1600s and 1900s that compiled all the formulas, like Newtown, Einstein, various chemists and scientists of that era, mainly because I found it very interesting learning all those formulas and principles at school. The early mountaineers and explorers also interest me.

Who has been your greatest inspiration?

When I think about the person who's had the greatest impact on me or who always brings me back down to earth and makes me feel better, I always think about my mum. She's very different from me in a lot of ways but she's just the best and always seems to say the right things.

I've never had a rock star poster on the wall or sports star poster. I'm not into using those people for inspiration. It's more about the day-to-day people you see around you or those people who have really had a struggle or a challenge who have overcome it with such positive energy. When I see those stories, they're the ones that are inspiring. People who have had real hardships and overcome them and then use themselves as role models and an inspiration to others. They are the truly great inspirational people.

What do you want to do when you grow up?

When I grow up, I just want to keep having fun and enjoying myself and making sure that whatever I do I can have a positive contribution to other people but also have fun at the same time.

In future, maybe my career will progress to higher levels in business to eventually reach CEO level. Right now I'm happy being General Manager of a mine site because I enjoy the responsibility of running the operation, the production, managing big budgets and interacting with people in a positive way. Another possibility for the future is to consider Non-Executive Director roles on Boards.

I used to set goal after goal and achieve them in a quick timeframe, but that has slowed down slightly as I've been happy going with the flow a bit and getting solid experience at General Manager level. I'm enjoying myself and getting that balance and still doing my travelling and keeping fit and healthy and doing the fun things I like to do.

Have you got any specific message that you want to give other women that want to get into the industry, to give them hope and inspiration?

There are two really important things; to be positive and be authentic.

Have a positive outlook – your attitude, what you say and your body language. A positive leader really makes a difference to the team. Make sure you do things that give you positive energy, that re-charge you up inside and keep your happy outlook.

Being authentic is so important, especially for women entering the industry. For example, when I was starting out in the industry back in the early '90s, it was a big drinking culture with lots of swearing and carrying on. I did feel the pressure to fit in, to drink beer and swear lots. After a short time I realised it wasn't me, I was starting to sound like someone I wasn't, and I didn't even like beer much.

It's important that women realise you don't have to change the person that you are to try to fit in or to live up to what you think might be the expectations of others. Just maintain yourself, your authenticity, your personality, principles and the character that you are. Being authentic develops trust and respect from others. It reduces stress, increases resilience, and makes us happier too, after all, there is nothing much more stressful than trying to be someone you're not.

Another key message is to 'go for it'. There will be challenges along the way. Work positively through them and ask for help from others when you need it. Make sure that others know your career aspirations so they can help you with them. Use role models and networking opportunities to help you out, and have courage to ask someone to be your mentor. Never be afraid to give something a go, even if you don't have the perfect experience for it.

Also for women entering the industry, it's important that we don't think that things should be different or harder because of gender. Don't think about barriers, think about getting on with the job. We need to work hard to deliver results for the business, demonstrate strong leadership and decision making, have an unwavering commitment to safety, and be recognised and promoted for those things.

Have you got any comments about women in the industry in general?

It would be great if we didn't have to have books like this. It would be great if we didn't have to have special women's networking events or special women's awards. We do need to keep encouraging and making a special effort but one day I'm hoping that over 45% of the workforce will be women in these types of industries. That recruitment of women into these industries is no longer an initiative but is part of the culture. That 'women in mining' is not a special subject any more, and it's normal to be a woman in resources. Where it's a natural choice for women in high school to choose these careers, and 50% of graduates and apprentices are women. It will be great when one day we don't have to have special initiatives for women because it's just a natural part of our culture.

My mentors and most of the people who have supported me through my career journey have been men. They have helped me get to where I am today through their support. Also, I'm responsible for over 2,000 men so the last thing I want is for people to think that I'm all about women. That would just totally disregard everything that I stand for. I have been asked many times to be involved in debates or give comments to the media about things that I don't agree with that would just spark a big debate about men versus women in the industry. I refuse to be involved with those topics. Obviously managing as many men as I do, I don't ever want to be seen as a big feminist or anything like that because I'm certainly not.

For me, it's about women delivering results for the business and being recognised for that, and encouraging women to have confidence and to 'give it a go'. That's what it's about. I agreed to be part of this book because of the concept. If what I have said encourages even a few women to get out there and 'give it a go', it's going to be worth it. I've had a great career and a lot of fun at the same time, and hopefully that's encouraging to others.

I've won quite a few business awards and got quite a lot of recognition because of my career success, but I like to stay humble and don't let it go to my head. I don't like to make a big deal of it, but if I can leverage off those things and help other women and inspire them, then that's what I should do, give back to others. I've mentored over 30 women across the industry and think it's really important to give back wherever I can.

I hope one day that the people I'm mentoring now will be able to do the same for others and it's just a never ending cycle.

> *"I build all of my businesses with clear systems because you should set your business up to sell."*
>
> **Sharon Jurd**
> **Australian Franchise Woman of the Year**

CHAPTER 10

Sharon Jurd

Franchise Woman of the Year
HydroKleen

CHAPTER 10

Sharon Jurd
Franchise Woman of the Year
HydroKleen

Sharon is a highly respected international best-selling author as well as a seasoned business executive, entrepreneur, growth strategist and success coach. She is passionate about helping people grow their business faster than the competition by giving those business owners financial freedom and the choice to live the life they deserve.

Sharon is qualified and recognised as a leading business coach, licensed business agent, licensed real estate agent, licensed auctioneer, licensed stock and station agent and she holds a diploma in business and franchising. Sharon's passion for peak performance and creating success started just six months after she opened her first real estate office as a Century 21 franchisee. She obtained a 72% market share despite having six major well established competitors. Within the year Sharon had opened her second office and quickly became a major player in that marketplace too – as the youngest single female director within the organisation. After dominating this area Sharon went looking for a new challenge and sold her successful awarding winning real estate offices. Sharon is the director of her own franchise network "HydroKleen Australia" and grew it enormously, making it the leader in its field.

What ignited the spark for what you're doing?

For me it has changed over the years. Initially, I wanted to own my own business. I had a business and it was growing at a fast rate which ignited the spark for what I do now, helping other people grow their businesses. I do that through a number of ways, in my approach, in my seminars and in my franchise company.

I had a range of ways of helping people at different levels in their business. I think that from what I expected, you have to get motivated to exercise but you have to exercise to get motivated.

Once I helped one person, I could see that I was actually helping someone which encouraged me to do more and more and I just kept saying to myself, "I want to do more and more of that" because it just feels good. It's heart-warming to me as well.

How would you define success?

Success is different for everyone but for me it's to love and to be loved. I think that if you have lots of love in your life you're pretty successful regardless of the material things and all of the achievements attain.
I think the definition of success changes through what you're doing and obviously that's life.

But the other areas of success change too. I think that it can just be amended by what you want to achieve. Sometimes you can be successful by just getting through one day.

Then another definition of success may be that you do start your own business and become an entrepreneur. So it does change through what you're doing.

"Make a moment, make a memory."

Heather Jones

Your firsthand experiences are key to what you're doing now. How has that changed?

It's pretty boring, Lynette. I wasn't all that entrepreneurial. You hear lots of successful people saying that they started out when they were nine or twelve but I don't have any recollection of having brilliant ideas and going out there and then hitting the money as a child. I went through school and I was very passionate about school and did well.

But I just worked and I got paid by the hour and it wasn't until later on that I realised that working per hour or getting paid per hour was not where I want to be long term. It wasn't until later that I went, "Oh no! There's something different out there for me."

What would be your most satisfying moment in your career?

The most satisfying happens quite regularly now but the most satisfying for me is when someone contacts me, whether it's by email, social media or in person and says that in some way I changed their life.

That's been my business, Sharon Jurd Events, because I wanted people who were in a pinch in life when they met me be able to say, "When I met Sharon, I learned something from her" or "I had a light bulb moment where there was a change in the direction or a change in my life." When people come up to share their journey with me it is absolutely satisfying.

How would you find people to bring into your business?

As an entrepreneur you'll realise it's very difficult to get people to be as passionate as you are but you can get people who really care about what you're doing and to bring some passion with it.

The way that I do that, is give them a really clear vision of what I want to achieve because if you give clarity to your team, then they'll get what you're trying to do and that brings the passion. But I think to find those people it's really on a referral basis, someone knows someone, rather than going out and finding them in the big wide world.

I think they come into your life when you put it out that you're looking for someone and when I'm looking for someone to join my team or my journey, I just tell everybody I know and they bring those people to me. Then you have to make sure that they have the same values and ideals as you about your business.

Is that similar to how you find your franchisees for HydroKleen?

Absolutely, our franchising in HydroKleen is close to 90%. 88% of our new franchises come from referrals because the team that we've got in our franchisees now, they're all different people but they're all the same. They still have the same values and they still have the same passions so they tell other people who have the same career in mind and passion and values. They always refer great people to us. Like-minded people hang around with like-minded people.

If you had the chance to start your career over again, what would you do differently?

I would own my own business earlier. Not that I was really that old but if I knew then what I know now I would have started a lot earlier and got my career underway and reaped the benefits of that early on.

What three pieces of advice would you give college students who want to be entrepreneurs?

Three pieces of advice would be:

1. Start early. Don't wait for everything to be right, it's never going to be perfect to start and when you start you won't know everything. I talked to a lot of people who are in business, entrepreneurs and they all say that when they started they knew nothing about what they were doing. Don't let that hold you back.

2. Hang around positive people. The friends that you keep should be moving forward, wanting to be entrepreneurs and owning their own business and being successful in their careers. It drives your motivation and it kicks you when you're supposed to keep up.

3. Find good mentors around you. When I was younger, I didn't see the importance of that. These people don't have to be someone that you know personally but with the technology of the internet now, they can be someone that you admire virtually and you can follow them in the virtual world and look to them if they're doing something similar to what you want to do. I have different mentors for different things. Look for someone who's doing what you want to achieve and then follow them and do what they're doing and it will make your journey a lot easier.

What are your ideals on life?

That's easy. I'm honest and that's first, above anything. I say it how it is and sometimes people don't like to hear the truth but I think that it's very important if you have a good relationship with that person. That they may not take it on board right away but they will go away and think about it.

It'd be nice, say my franchisees or the people I coach and the people that come to my seminars when I tell them, "If it's going to be hard, it's going to be hard." I don't pretend that this journey is easy.

What I do is tell it like it is and I keep it very simple for people. So it's that honesty about the journey, going, "All right, the next three weeks for example, you're going to have to work your butt off" and I explain what they need to do. I'm very honest about it. I don't gloss over it and tell them everything is going to be okay when it really may not be.

Do you see a difference between people who are entrepreneurs and people who work for someone else?

Absolutely, without a doubt. It can even be within yourself. I proved this with myself. I worked for a gentleman for many years who I absolutely respected and I managed his businesses. I was a signature on the cheque book and I had absolute freedom to run that business and I grew it from a team of two people in itself up to a team of twelve people and a national franchise company; it dominated the market.

I did everything that I was expected to as a manager but when I left and became my own business owner I realised there was a lot more that I could have been doing.

Once you own your own business and become that entrepreneur within yourself, you will work a hundred times harder than you would for somebody else. The main reason for that is your passion.

You're building yourself up and a lot of the time the spirit of value as well. It's that passion about what you're doing because most of the time when you work for somebody else, it's not your passion, it's somebody else's passion and once you get to your passion and doing your own thing you're a completely different person.

You have had some valuable challenges, what have you learned from them?

I've had a number of challenges. Early on, my biggest challenge was being quite direct with my team and really not appreciating what they were doing for me. It took me a long time to learn that. It was my way or the highway. I didn't communicate with them very well about my direction or where I wanted to end up. I expected them to follow me and understand what I was all about.

So I had to really change that and bring the team into my world. Get them into my head so they could try and understand what was ticking over in there but once I started to do that they got on-board the train with me and said, "Yup, we're on it with you" and I really invited them to be a part of that journey. Now I have what we call, alignment day, so they can get in alignment with me and I keep them informed about what I want to do.

Then we can just go away and do what needs to be done and make those deadlines and reach those goals. So, I think the biggest challenge for me was turning around my attitude of going, "Okay, this is a team effort here. It's not me having you follow along and do what I need you to do."

Do you think that was one of your greatest fears?

I've always wanted to get things done and I needed a really fast pace so I knew the time to slow down would have helped them keep up with me because my greatest fear is that life's short and I've got a lot to do and I want to achieve a lot of things. Not on a day to day basis. I'm talking like big picture stuff.

So I've got to keep doing it and it's not all work. I've got personal stuff that I want to achieve as well. So I was just moving too fast and I was allowing these people to catch up. My biggest fear was that I was going to sit on my rocking chair on the front porch saying, "Look at all the things I should've done." That's scary.

What do you consider to be your greatest achievement and what is the single most important reason for your success?

I think for me, I had lots of small achievements with certain people and all of that sort of thing but for me personally, I love awards. Some people say, "Oh, that's a bit materialistic" but it's not really, it's just a chance for me to say, "You know, I'm on the right track and someone is giving me a pat on the back."

When you're an entrepreneur in business on your own the only person that's patting you on the back is you and it can feel lonely at times. So when I have the opportunity to win an award, I just embrace that as a great achievement.

Being the one that was awarded when I was in real estate and that was in the top 2% worldwide. It sort of makes you stop and reflect and go, "I'm doing a really good job here" and thankfully I'm being recognised for that.

I just recently won Franchise Woman of the Year for Australia and again, it was like, "Oh my God!" I'm out there slogging it every day. As some people say, "When you're working hard you've got your head down, bum up" but when that award pops up in front of you, sometimes unannounced, you go, "Oh my God, I am making a difference in people's lives. I am doing what I want to do and I am achieving the things that I want to achieve."

How has being an entrepreneur affected your family life?

Early on it was pretty tough because I was a single mother of two with two real estate offices, so my personal life went out the window during those times but I really changed my peace and live around that work/life balance. I don't like that terminology too much but that's what it is. Now I have a real balance around what I do but when you start a new business, it takes you a little time to get that balance. If you put the foundation team in the business early on then you will get that balance more quickly and I think now that I have a really good family life and I get to spend a lot of time with my partner, John.

We travel and do a lot of things that I love to do but I must admit to your readers out there that there are times when it gets tough being an entrepreneur and trying to juggle all the vessels at once.

What does a day in the life of Sharon Jurd consist of?

I wake up at 4am every morning. Frankly, I'm at my best when I'm up early. I say to people, "If you send me an email at 4:30am, you'll get a response but at 4:30pm most likely because I'm not clocking off first for the day."

I get up and I always take time for myself first because it's quiet and my mind is not cluttered with the busyness of the day. So some mornings I have a personal trainer who comes around and I exercise. I always take my time and I grab a green tea and I go outside and stand in the garden for a few minutes. I just bring myself into a calm state because I know that during the day it can get very hectic.

I just make sure that I'm very level headed before I start my day. Even if it's just a couple of hours you get before everybody else wakes up you can get a lot of stuff done and I achieve the things that I need to get off my plate because they might take a lot of brain power from me so I get them out of the way early on.

If I have to go and meet people and network or go to meetings I tend to do them in the afternoon when I can sit down and have a cup of tea and relax a little bit more.

"Marvellous Monday
Terrific Tuesday
Wonderful Wednesday
Thoughtful Thursday
Fabulous Friday
Safety Saturday
Safety Sunday
No matter what sort of day you are having, there is
no reason why you cannot greet someone with this
attitude."

Heather Jones

What would be the strangest thing that you've done in your lifetime?

I've jumped out of a plane, twice.

The first time I jumped out of the plane was at Coffs Harbour on that main coast and the second time I landed on Pure Beach on the Queensland, south coast. I apparently, stupidly, said to my partner that I would do it all again in a heartbeat.

So he made sure that for my 40th birthday he got my ticket and jumped out of the way. So, I haven't said it again but that was strange for me. I never wanted to jump out of a plane, it was never something that I longed to do.

Both times it was unannounced and I just went and did it. But if anybody ever gets the opportunity to go and do a cannon skydive, just go and do it because once you do that you think that you're bullet-proof.
It doesn't matter what happens in your business, as tough as it might get, you say, "I jumped out of a plane. I have nothing to fear" and nothing's ever a problem anymore. Nothing gets you frazzled and you're so motivated to achieve things.

What would you say are the five key elements to starting and running a business or businesses?

My biggest passion, which I'll put at number one, has to be systems. I build all of my businesses with clear systems because I always say that you should set your business up to sell.

Now, you may not be wanting to sell it and you may think you'll do it for the rest of your life but at some point, you may want to retire and sell it.

The other thing is that you may become unwell and need to sell it quite quickly. What happens with the systems is that your team runs the systems and the systems run the business.

When you've got systems in place it cuts down on all the training of your staff. You don't have to be there to do it. Someone else can do it and your business runs extremely smoothly. So that's my first one and I can talk for an hour on systems but I'll move on.

Number two, my team; you choose your team very well. And as I said earlier, bring those passionate people on board with you that really want to take your success and you can make them successful along the way. Number three, make sure that you know your ideal customer; get a real clear picture. Where do they hang out? What do they do? What are their fears? Why do they lie awake at night? What do they spend their money on?

So you can really understand who you're going to market to because you can't go out and market to everyone. I had a broker say once, "Oh, I market to everyone that's got a house." No, that's not what you need to do. You need to narrow that ideal customer down. Quite narrow so you can understand where you've got to market and what language you need to talk to them.

Number four would be, have a very clear vision on what you want to achieve. Everyone wants to earn money but if you're just in it for the money you're not going to be successful. You need to remember that most people want to help others get rid of a pain of some sort so you think about why you are in this and what you want to achieve in the long term and make sure everybody knows it.

And the last, but definitely not least, would have to be passion. If you're not passionate about it, you will not grow your business as fast or as successfully as you'd hoped. If you're not passionate about it, get off the train and get on the pony that you are passionate about. Don't jump into a business just because you think it's a money making machine because that money will dry up. The passion will bring the money for you.

"Giving up on your goal because of one setback is like slashing your other three tyres because you got a flat."

Unknown

On the subject of money, how would you obtain business for any of your ventures?

A referral option is always the way I've gone. I haven't had too many investors coming to my business but I have my newest business that's about to be released this year and I needed quite a large investor. And it came, and again, I just put it out there to the people that I thought would know people and the universe brought me that person so I didn't have to go out to the big wide world to find them. Yes, definitely tell everybody that you're looking for someone and they'll find someone for you.

Is there some pattern or formula to becoming successful?

Two words that I like to use: consistency and persistency. So you've got to be consistent. People will start with one thing and then it dies off. When people come to my one-on-one coaching program I ask them if they are doing a certain thing and they say, "Oh, I used to but I don't anymore" and I say to them, "Well, why not?" so they say, "I don't know." So that's consistency. Once you start something, I say that you should never stop. You can change or you can change your direction but you don't stop, you keep going until that's no longer working for you and the consistency with getting the right team members or getting the right clients. I've got a chart where it shows people who tried to get a new client once or twice and then they gave up. If that happens, you turn outside as an excuse instead of looking within. You have to keep building that relationship and keep going back to those clients and customers for the longer term, to get those A-clients around you.

Looking back, what would be the one thing you wish you understood about entrepreneurship before you ever got started?

I think for me it was that I'm good enough to do it. I was always waiting to learn more, do more or have more knowledge. You know, "I've only been in the industry for this long... I only know this market place" and that, I think, holds a lot of people back saying, "Who am I to be an all-star? There are a lot more people out there that know a lot more than me." But the thing is that you don't have to know as much as them because there's a lot of people who don't know as much as you and once I realised that I have something to give to people and I could change their lives, it changed my life.

If you could offer an entrepreneur one piece of advice, what would it be?

Don't have a plan B. So when you go in and you get started you go, "I'm in. I'm jumping in. I'm not putting my pony out and seeing if it works. I'm going in and I don't have a plan B. I have to make this work." And you will make it work because your passion will drive you but if you go, "Oh, I'm just going to do this and if it doesn't go well, I'll do that" then it won't go well. You've got to go in having no plan B. In all of my businesses I don't have a plan B so it has to work and once you have got rid of that plan B you will make it work and it will work easily.

Do you have a business idea that you will never ever use?

If you're talking about inventing something, I've come up with these great ideas and then I realise I'm really behind the times. The thing that I wanted to really develop was a waterproof notepad for the shower and then I went to a conference and saw that they're actually doing it online via emails on these shower things. So I thought I was a little bit behind the times but I always need a notepad in my shower and I really wanted a waterproof one that I could take with me afterwards. So that's my idea and I'll probably never ever use it because the technology is going to overtake me before I ever get to design one.

If you could talk to one person from history, who would it be and why?

I think it would be Marilyn Monroe because she kept her self-confidence and that self- image and I think that from a woman's perspective you need to be comfortable in your own skin and with your own body-image. She was a size 14 I believe and at the time that was large. She didn't care. She loved her body and obviously flaunted it. I'd really like to get inside of her head and ask, "Why do we women have so many hang-ups about our body?"

Who has been your greatest inspiration?

There have been many, I must admit and as I've gone through the journey, when I was wanting to achieve a certain thing, I would draw inspiration from different people. I think of the people who are around me now, one is Darren Stevens and I know that you know him and I have for years. He gives me great inspiration in the sense that, when I was becoming an author he was already an author of multiple books and I really wanted him to show me how to do this and do it well. And also, in the marketing arena, he helps me with my marketing and my direction and my clarity about what I want to achieve. He's very business minded and keeps me on track in that area. In my personal life, and even though she's business based, there's another lady called Karen Scott. I always say that when I feel scared I talk to Karen because she lets me know that I don't need to be scared. But when I'm about to do something and I say, "Oh, this is scary stuff" Karen says, "What are you thinking Sharon? You've done so many businesses before, why are you scared of this one?" and she lets me know that I am capable of doing what I need to do. We all have fears along the way but fears just get bigger and so, just as a side note, when you're starting to become an entrepreneur and you have fears when you start, that fear will be the smallest fear you ever have because as you get bigger and do bigger things, you have bigger fears. They don't go away. You just learn that stuff's part of the journey and you get to understand it and enjoy it. Karen and I get on and hook up, she's based in New Zealand, and we laugh at ourselves and have a great joke about all the little things that we do and all of the exciting things that are happening and she just helps me not be scared.

Do you have a favourite book or what is your favourite? I imagine you have several.

Yes, the one that I love the most is a book called, "Stepping Up" by John Izzo. I read a lot of books; I get secrets out that have changed my life. This is a total mindset change for me and I have it on audio and I enjoy it over and over again because every time I listen to it I get something else out of it. If you haven't read that book, read it first, especially if you're just starting out.

What do you want to do when you grow up?

When I grow up, there are lots of things that I want to achieve. I have a hundred and one things that I want to achieve and there's still a lot on there but one of the things that I've always wanted to be good at is singing and I can't sing. I'd be starting from the absolute bottom and as I slowdown in my business and enter older age, I'm going to take singing lessons. I don't have to sing in front of large crowds but strive for excellence might get me there but I just want to be able to sing.

Where do you see yourself and your business in 10 or 20 years?

I have a really clear vision about what I want to achieve and I can I see it with clarity and I think that's important for people. If you get that clarity, it will happen. I want to be working at helping people grow their businesses and change their life because that's what I do. I go to people and I ask, "What do you want to achieve personally? Let's make your business achieve that." So even though I'm coming from a business perspective, put your systems in place and know your ideal customer. I'm doing that so they can achieve the things personally and that's how I run my businesses. The thing that I love to do the most is travel because there's a big wide world out there and you just learn so much from different cultures and experiences. Of course, I'm also a foodie and I love to eat different foods from different cultures. I did it twofold because I'm helping people grow their business and this is when they're in their own right and achieve their personal things. That gives me the luxury of then being able to travel and get out and see those people and talk to them in different countries.

CHAPTER II

Photographer Tony McDonagh

Heather Jones

Pilbara Heavy Haulage Girls
Western Australia

CHAPTER 11

Heather Jones
Pilbara Heavy Haulage Girls
Western Australia

Today Tonight - Women in Trucks – 2014 – Seven Network
Today Tonight – Truckie Lyndal – 2014 – Seven Network
The Project – 2015 – Southern Cross Ten
2015 ATA Top Industry Award
"Most Outstanding Contribution to the Australian Trucking Industry Award,"

Heather Jones is a madly passionate woman. She is also Managing Director of Success Transport and CEO of Pilbara Heavy Haulage Girls – based in the Pilbara region Western Australia. When her marriage ended in the mid 90's Heather found herself with three daughters to raise on her own. Looking to find work that would enable this doting Mum to spend as much time with her girls as she could, a friend offered Heather the opportunity to drive one of his trucks whilst having the girls with her on the proviso that her daughter did not get out of the truck at any stage on any job.

That single act of kindness changed her life. She home-schooled her girls and brought them up in the truck through necessity. Heather's resilience is extraordinary. She has faced some daunting setbacks in her life but has always been resolute that she can and will survive anything. Heather's vision is to change the way the general public perceive truck drivers and through advocacy, mentoring, training and education right across the Australian road transport industry, in schools, prisons, media and government departments. As CEO of Pilbara Heavy Haulage Girls and full time driver Heather oversees a unique educational enterprise that heralds a quantum leap in terms of how heavy vehicles drivers are trained. She is recognised nationally for her amazing work.

What ignited the spark for the love of what you do?

Quite simply, the need to feed and support my three daughters.

Something that was born out of necessity has turned into my life passion – something that I love and I get paid for it!

I just love our industry. There is so much that needs to be changed. At industry conference recently, I diplomatically pointed out to the blokes that they'd been the industry caretakers for the past 100 years and that perhaps some female input was needed to steer it in a new direction.

What has been the most satisfying moment in your career?

Every time one of my student drivers completes their training and moves into employment. These are the high points of the work I do, knowing also their new employer has a trained, professional, safety conscious driver behind the wheel of their truck. That is so satisfying. This training is done at no cost to self-funded drivers.

I placed my 33rd student driver with a transport company two weeks ago. Within a week of completing training, I am delighted to say that every single student I've worked with has secured full-time employment. Pilbara Heavy Haulage Girls now have over 500 newly licensed drivers including a number of men on local, state and national waiting lists eagerly waiting for a call from the west to commence their 160 hours heavy vehicle driver boot-camp.

Students work in diverse and challenging live work environments under the supervision of myself or any of PHHG's other professional heavy vehicle drivers. Whilst some classroom time is required in the classroom, the bulk of the 160 hours is done on-the-job. This gives both students and trainers the opportunity to see if a career truck driving is for them.

We've been approached by a number of major national trucking companies interested in placing our graduates on completion of their 160 hours training. Once employed, graduates will ideally commence a Certificate III in Transport and Logistics with their new employers – the end result being well rounded, skilled, professional, safety conscious Australian heavy vehicle drivers.

What was your first entrepreneurial experience as a kid?

As a child, I would go picking strawberries at the age of 14 just out of Bunbury in Western Australia. I'd jump out of bed at 4 in the morning, wait for my lift at the front gate and we'd do the 30km trip to the strawberry farm every morning before school. In winter, I'd be freezing cold and soaking wet but the $12 I earned each pay day made it all worthwhile.

How have your entrepreneurial motivations changed since you first started doing what you're doing now?

Whilst I still get up at 4am most mornings and am constantly seeking ways to improve the industry, the $$$'s I earn these days are thankfully more than the $12 I earned picking strawberries - a large portion of which is ploughed back into the industry for student training.

When I entered the industry 20 years ago, female drivers were few and far between. Whilst things have improved to a degree, industry take-up has been slow with female heavy vehicle driver participation rates still quite low. These days I focus on working to balance the gender scales, in addition to educating all road users on how to share our roads safely.

How do you find people to bring into your business that actually care about the business the way you do?

During the interview process, we endeavour to establish whether staff have the right aptitude and on-road attitude. If they demonstrate an eagerness to contribute to the business, rather than just looking for what's in the job for them, i.e. "what can I do for you?" not "what's in it for me?" then they're the staff we'll employ every time.

If you had your chance to start your career over again, what would you do differently?

I would hire a big, burly debt collector and get him to go and chase my debts after 14 days. Non-payment for work done is far too common in the industry, particularly for owner drivers – those least able to afford hefty losses.

I nearly went under in my business at the end of 2009 because I had three of my client companies went into receivership and three didn't pay - because they too had not been paid. When you don't have money for legal fees to chase the bills, you just can't get your money. It's a vicious cycle.

What three pieces of advice would you give to college students who want to be truck drivers and want to be business owners in the transport industry?

Firstly, I would recommend that those considering becoming an owner/driver do a small business course and maybe certificate III in Transport and Logistics.

Secondly, I believe its vital students find at least 2 industry mentors, drivers they look up to and drivers they can call on for advice and guidance.

Finally, where possible, I would advise owner drivers to try to find a niche market within the industry where they can provide new service in the region so they're not competing with every other transport company in the area for the same work.

What are your ideals?

Always be positive and happy, always.

Even if you've had a bad day, your body doesn't know it so if you smile it still releases endorphins. Surround yourself with supportive people and always remember, one person can change the world.

And if you don't think one person can change the world, when you go to sleep at night and that mosquito comes into your bedroom and buzzes around your head, believe me - that can change your world.

How do you find a mentor for yourself? You're mentoring girls and other women but you need support for yourself as well. So where do you go to find that?

My mentors are all male truck drivers, men who have been in the industry for a very, very long time. Early 2015, I spoke at an Industry conference on the importance of gender diversity and training in the road transport sector. As I talked, scanning the room I made eye contact with three of my mentors, all men, scattered through the crowd. All three were sitting there with beaming smiles on their faces and I knew all of them were proud of me, proud of the work I do and proud of how I now mentor others – as they had mentored me.

With regard to my personal life, I have 3 beautiful daughters and 3 close girlfriends – all right there day OR night if I need to some advice or just to talk.

In developing and establishing Pilbara Heavy Haulage Girls, my business partner and I have looked long and hard for people with the same passion, focus and drive to join us on our journey to transform the way heavy vehicle driver training is delivered. As such, we now have a Board of competent, skilled professionals - experienced in transport and logistics, business development, and training and recruitment.

What do you feel is the major difference between the people who have an entrepreneurial mind and someone who wants to work for someone else?

When you work for someone else, there are too many roadblocks to be able to make change but when you work for yourself – you can change the World! People with entrepreneurial minds are always for new ways to streamline processes and promote their business and industry by working smarter not harder. Entrepreneurial people recognise staff are their most valuable asset and as such encourage full participation in research, development and change. Entrepreneurial people encourage staff and stakeholders to look at things differently - to embrace change.

What have you learned most from your challenges?

I've learned that when you do stand up and speak out, often you find you're not alone.

I've learned that what doesn't kill you will make you stronger.

I've learned that sometimes just focusing on the next minute or the next five minutes is what will get you through.

I've learnt from my challenges that sharing ideas with the wrong people can mean losing everything.

I've learned to walk away from negative people as no matter how strong you are they will work to chip away at your energy and finally

I've learned it's very easy to stand by and criticise but takes great strength to stand up when others won't.

So what's your greatest fear and how do you manage it?

My greatest fear is to see the industry continue on exactly the same as it's done for the last 100 years, rather than keep pace with a rapidly changing world. My greatest fear is that I will continue to see our wonderful truck drivers ducking behind bushes on the sides of highways due to lack of toilet facilities, dying needlessly due to risks taken on our roads by uneducated motorists and being screwed down to their last $ by unscrupulous multi-nationals working to build shareholder dividends.

In terms of managing these injustices, I work with my team to lobby all three tiers of government and industry stakeholders – often taking the decision makers in my truck on long-haul trips so they can experience first-hand the third world conditions drivers are forced to work under. I find enabling them to experience the journey rather than just talking about it over a cappuccino in an air-conditioned office with executive washrooms close by is most effective.

> *"If you need somebody to talk to, source it out. Don't think that if you start your time and you're struggling that it's going to get better or you're just going to quit. Actually speak to somebody because that could be the difference between finishing your apprenticeship or not."*
>
> *Helen Yost*
> *Plumber*

What would you consider to be your greatest achievement and what's the single most important reason for that success?

My greatest achievement is having three beautiful, well-balanced children that are productive in society.

What would you say are the 5 key elements for starting and running a successful business?

Know your stuff.

Know your clients.

Choose staff wisely.

Know the politics of the industry

Employ a skilled financial advisor who has extensive industry experience and knowledge

How do you go about marketing your business?

We have developed our Pilbara Heavy Haulage Girls brand around our amazing female heavy vehicle drivers – showcasing the challenging work these amazing women do in trying conditions, always laughing, despite the relentless dust, extreme heat and flies.

Given our girls drive the largest on-road truck combinations in the world, media and readers and viewers world-wide eagerly consume articles and stories from the road and the lives of the Pilbara Heavy Haulage Girls. Our Facebook page and website are updated constantly with stories and photos from out where the rubber hits the road and we are constantly in contact with media announcing milestones in our business development.

We are fortunate to enjoy strong relationships with local, state, national and international journalists who regularly phone, seeking reports on our progress as we develop a model that represents a major shift in the way training is delivered in the Australian road transport sector.

Looking back, what's one thing you wish you'd understood about business and entrepreneurship before you ever got started?

If you decide to go down that pathway, choose your business partners wisely. Look for those who share your passion, have a strong moral compass, high ethical standards and a proven track record.

When you grow up, what do you want to be?

I think I'd like to be a grey nomad, travelling the roads at 40kms an hour, setting up camp each night in one of the very few truck bays along the highways with all my other grey nomad friends. As a kind person, I'd send a friendly wave to all the truckies honking their horns as they drive past appreciating that friendly one-finger salute they all seem to do out the window. (Just JOKING!!!)

No really …. when I grow up, what do I want to be? ….. Quite simply, proud of all those professional heavy vehicle drivers out there working hard to change the face of the industry through engaging in responsible driving, safe work practices, high personal presentation standards, mentoring newly licensed drivers and treating all road users with courtesy, understanding and respect.

CHAPTER 12

Helen Yost

Plumber

Queensland

CHAPTER 12

Helen Yost
Plumber
Queensland

Certificate III in Sanitary Plumbing, Drainage and Gasfitting.

Helen was working in Administration for a plumbing business but wanted desperately to be a Qualified Plumber and after convincing her then boss to let her try it – she succeeded.   In 2010 she started a solely female plumbing business "The Plumbettes" and has 2 girls. This is how she juggles her professional and family life.

Why did you want to be a plumber and what ignited this spark to create that passion?

It's a bit of a funny story actually. I was originally a personal trainer being quite active and quite fit. I had two kids and then didn't have clientele to go back to because nobody wanted a fat personal trainer.

I went back to office work and I got a job with a plumbing company and I was the office manager but within six weeks I was bored of sitting at a desk. I said to my boss that I didn't really enjoy sitting at a desk and wasn't there something I could do like go out on site or something.

He said I could go out and do the monthly site inspections for the project clients. I said, "Oh, fantastic!" That was probably the worst thing he ever did though because once I was on site and I saw it, I said, "Oh my

God, this is so much fun."

Then I asked him, can I work on site with the boys? Can I have a go? And he said, "No." So I asked, "Why not?" And he said, "Girls don't plumb." I was stunned and said, "Excuse me?" And he repeated, "Girls don't plumb." I said, "Yes they do." But he was firm and said, "No, they don't and no, you're not going on site, sorry."

The next time we did project claims I was out on site and while my boss was down in a meeting with the other site managers I got talking to the boys and I asked, "What are you doing and why are you doing it that way? Why not this way or this way or this way?" And they told me, "Oh, because of this, this and this."

They explained it to me and I asked, "Oh, can I have a go?" Then one of the guys thought it would be really, really funny if I had a go but I actually did it right and he was surprised and it went from there. I thought, "Yeah, I really want to do this" and my boss came around the corner and he said, "You really are persistent aren't you?" And I replied, "Yes, I am."

So that's what started the spark but it was a good three years before I got my apprenticeship signed up. He still firmly believed that females don't plumb.

How do you balance your family life and being a trade person?

The beauty of having the Plumbettes is that I can work around my family life and still bring other girls into the business and get them doing what they love doing as well.

With regards to family life, I'm quite blessed in the sense that my step-daughter who's sixteen and incredibly independent, doesn't like anyone else cooking so she does all the cooking. She's probably one of those rare teenagers who is very mature for their age.

I'm very blessed in that I probably don't have the same struggles as a lot of other women might. I'm not saying that it's easy, it's definitely not the easiest thing, but I'm just like any other working mum in any industry. There's always going to be a struggle to balance work life with family life. So I guess my struggle is the same as anyone else's.

What has been your greatest successful moment in your workplace?

I'm going to say my most rewarding moment would have been when I employed my apprentice, Brittany. Knowing her background story and what she had to go through with her previous employer, was not pleasant at all.

She left the industry. She wasn't going to come back into it but then she found the Plumbettes and she actually contacted me to have a meeting. She just wanted to speak to somebody who's been in the industry and knows what it's about and what it's like and see whether she wanted to come back to it. When we spoke to her it was quite clear that she was very passionate about what she wanted to do and she's got the same passion and drive as me.

Giving her the opportunity to complete her apprenticeship in a supportive and encouraging environment is probably one of the reasons why I started it. To be able to fulfil it from the get-go is really awesome.

What has been your strangest job situation?

I don't know which one to pick, there are too many of them. I'd have to go with this gentleman who called us out. He was an elderly gentleman and he called because my partner is a plumber as well and the number connected to the Plumbettes was for his previous company. So he called that number and booked a job not realising that he'd called the Plumbettes.

When I got out there, he said, "You're not who I called." I replied, "No, but we're still plumbers." He's said, "Really??"
"Yup, yup, yup. We're definitely plumbers." He said, "Well that's awesome." He's a gentleman who would be in his eighties but he was speaking like a 30 year old. I thought, "That is so cool." And then once we did the job for him, he said, "You know, I've never had a plumber that's so polite and I've never had a plumber come in and I don't have to clean up after them and it was quite pleasant. Generally it's quite stressful to deal with, but no, this has been a wonderful experience." I replied, "Yeah, that's pretty cool." We've been back to do quite a few jobs for him. He's definitely a funny character.

"You are treated differently but usually once guys get to know you they are fine with it. Everyone will say, "You are just one of the boys."

Naomi Williams

Have you been treated differently because you are a woman?

Yes, there's no two ways about it. Even through TAFE I was treated differently.

In regards to TAFE, it was different with each teacher. Some teachers, like the teachers I got along well with, surprisingly, were the ones that treated me the same as they treated the boys. There was no increased expectation or decreased expectation. It was just, "You're in this and you're doing it the same as the boys."

They're the ones I got along with but some teachers expected more from me, intellectually, than the others did but then others expected less from me when I was actually on the tools and I told them, "Well no, I'm here to prove myself as a tradesperson. I don't want you to go easy on me because I'm a female and I don't have the same matching bits as you." But yeah, definitely, they definitely do treat you differently and even, ironically, the ladies treat you differently, which is surprising.

Some of them get really excited but there have been a couple that I've come across who have said, "Well, I didn't call a female, I called a male." "Well, actually you called the Plumbettes." "Yeah, but that's only a company run by females." I replied, "No, we're a company full of female plumbers." Then she said, "Oh, okay, okay, I guess you can do this job but I'll get a normal plumber next time." I responded with, "We are normal plumbers."

What final words have you got to say to inspire other people to come into the plumbing trade?

Follow your heart and don't take no for an answer because if I took no for an answer, there's no way I'd have the Plumbettes.

If you need somebody to talk to, source it out. Don't think that if you start your time and you're struggling that it's going to get better or you're just going to quit. Actually speak to somebody because that could be the difference between finishing your apprenticeship or not.

CHAPTER 13

Naomi Williams
Industrial Electrician

CHAPTER 13

Naomi Williams
Industrial Electrician

Naomi is an Industrial Electrician who has worked for several major companies including WorkPac in Darymple Bay Coal Terminal, Downer at Hay Point, SKM, Transfield, Fluor Global Services, Corke, Silcar and Thiess throughout Australia and is currently in North Queensland. Some of the amazing projects that she has worked have included HPX3 at Hay Point, Sarina Water Treatment Plant, Desalination Plant Wonthaggi, an numerous small projects at Loy Yang Mine, Hazelwood Power Station, Hamilton Iluka Mineral Sands and Maryvale Papermill. The project that has given her the greatest satisfaction was when she worked on Basslink for Siemens/ IMS.

Naomi is currently on Maternity Leave with her 2nd bub.

What ignited your initial passion to want to be an industrial electrician?

I did my VCE and had no idea what I wanted to do so I had a few temporary jobs out of high school and a couple were typical female dominated secretary roles etc. but one I started was a circuit board. I was building circuit boards assembly for veterinary equipment and while I love that, it was still in an office, which I didn't want.

I wanted to get out there and see the other end of how these circuit boards were working and the guy that I spoke to, who I was working for at the time, said, "Maybe electrical would be something for you." So I pursued that for probably 12 months until I got an apprenticeship and then went from there. I have been fully qualified since 2005.

What would be the most successful moment you can recall in your work place?

As I'm an industrial electrician and I've never done any sort of domestic work so I've always set goals for myself to get on large scale construction jobs because my favourite part of work is to do construction. I've managed to break into the industry which is actually quite hard to get into as there tends to be what they call in the industry, the purple circle, and there is the chosen crew of guys that always get the construction jobs.

Breaking into that purple circle is hard enough for anyone, let alone a female electrician, so I'm always quite proud of myself when I get onto another one of those jobs. I always call it my dream job and I seem to finish one and create the next dream job that I'm going to chase then.
Okay, probably my very first one. So I had just finished my electrical apprenticeship and I got onto the Bass Link Project, which connects electricity between Tasmania and Victoria and that's done via a massive sub-sea cable that was dropped between the two. So that was my very first job and that was the initial excitement that got me thinking that this is something that I want to keep doing.

The cable is classified as the largest sub-sea HV-DC connector cable in the southern hemisphere which is, if you're an electrician, impressive. Anyone else would be blasé about it.

What's been your strangest job or the strangest situation you've found yourself in?

It was something simple like having to change the exhaust fans in the male locker room or shower room while guys were coming in dripping wet or wanting to have a shower because they were wet and dirty from work. We had a laugh about it and I said, "Don't worry, I've seen it all before."

I have worked with a lot of strange characters in my time that left me thinking, "I don't know if I want to be working with this person."

One of the strangest things I've had to do is work with four other females and it was hilarious. I was working in a workshop with four others, three female electricians and one female T.A. and there must have been 20 guys or about 20 workers all up in the workshop but it was like the tables were turned because we were the intimidating bunch and they couldn't handle us giggling away in the corner and making remarks.

I never get to work with so many females in one place but it was fabulous, so I keep in touch with all of them. Female tradies are all very similar. The more you talk to people from other trades the more you see it. I think we've just all got, I don't know, maybe not a personality type but it definitely takes a certain type of lady to be able to fulfil this role and you make lifetime friends with those people too.

Have you been treated differently because you are a woman and why do you think so, whether it's yes or no?

I'd definitely say you're treated differently. I think people will set you a task. Not to see if you fail but to see if you pass. Every time I start with a new crew of guys they all sort of do this. Maybe they're not sure if I'm going to be able to fit in with them so they sort of set a test. I don't think it's to make you fail or anything but I always prove them wrong and that's a little bit of job satisfaction in itself. So you are treated differently and when you work with some older gentlemen and they think, "I'll have to carry the ladder for her because she can't carry the ladder" or that sort of thing and I usually have to set them straight. Yeah, so I guess you are treated differently but usually once guys get to know you they are fine with it. Everyone will say, "You are just one of the boys, Naomi."

They all say, "She's just one of the boys" or if there have been jobs where I've spent a lot of time with people they just treat you like their sister or annoying wife. I've been called the work wife occasionally.

How do you balance your family life and being a tradesperson?

That's been the toughest thing yet. The job that I'm currently on at the moment, I do eight hour days on Mondays and Fridays and I do nine hour days on Tuesdays, Wednesdays and Thursdays but I don't work on the weekend. The job that I had three months prior to that, I was doing seventy hours a week and I'd do two weeks of seventy hours a week, so 10 hour days and I get one day off and then I'd get a week off after four weeks. So it's been tough. It's not a trade where you can get an opportunity to work part time. I think if I could work three days a week, I'd love to, just because I do have a son who has just turned two and I feel like I miss him quite a bit. But we manage.

We moved up here away from family, so I don't have family to baby-sit or anything. He's in family day care but having said that, whenever I've had to take sick days because he's been sick, everyone has been okay and I was worried about it because I thought I was going to get the comment, "You're a mum, you should be at home looking after him."

But they've all been completely understanding about it and a lot of them have said to me, "I don't know how you do it" because they've got young kids themselves and they just say, "Oh, I totally understand, you need to be with your son today." I've had no backlash from it at all, so that's been very good.

I think everyone's compassionate and I think anyone that's got kids or had kids, they understand because they've all been there. They all know that you just have to do what you have to do. I've been fortunate so far, and look, I've only had a few jobs since I've had Olly but everyone has been quite good about it so far.

My mum was a nurse and she probably worked very similar hours to what I'm doing. You know, she had to do night shifts and long day shifts and all of that and to be honest, I think that's where I get my work ethic from. She worked really hard for us kids.

"Do today what you want to be remembered for tomorrow."

Stephen Parr
Author
Take Charge of Your Money Now

ABOUT THE AUTHOR

Lynette Gray

Entrepreneur, International Author, Investor, Traveller

Lynette is a seasoned entrepreneur, international author, investor and traveller. Born into a family of entrepreneurs, she was destined to make an impact on the business world.

She grew up on a grain property in the country and was happiest working alongside her father, either in the shed or out in the paddock. Years later, she assisted her parents with their road-train business transporting cattle and grain.

Before launching her own business, Lynette worked hard at developing a broad range of business skills in a variety of industries. She started her working life designing and fitting out brides and bridesmaids and then worked in administration, finance, production and sales roles which developed her into a well-rounded entrepreneur with a keen perspective on business management.

Lynette ran Kwik 'n' Kool Refrigerated Couriers from her home while raising her three sons. She fondly recalls mornings when the truck drivers sat around the kitchen table while the boys got ready for school. She generated sales and built the business from behind a steering wheel. After growing the business from one truck to five vehicles in three years, and relocating to a new depot facility, the business started to fail.

Undeterred, Lynette always believed in her vision, so she refocused and rebuilt it.

Her prestigious list of customers includes major brands such as, Simon Transport, McNab Constructions, Success Craft Skiboats, Manassen Foods, Vic's Meats, Cadbury's, Golden Cockerel, Bidvest, QFFS, Beak A La Carte, Australian Bakels and Le Cake. She also services prestigious restaurants including Aria, Cha Cha Char, The Hilton in Brisbane and Surfers Paradise.

She is a member of the Queensland Transport Association, Transport Women Australia, Safe Food Queensland, the Australian Businesswomen Network, Qld Rural, Regional & Remote Womens Network, Surat Basin Enterprise and the Queensland Chamber of Commerce. Her business skills have been recognised by several organisations. She was a winner of the AIM Queensland Management Excellence Award and she was a finalist for the Heritage Business Award in the Business and Professional category.

She has travelled and worked throughout New Zealand, Hong Kong, Thailand and China.

Lynette Gray is the author of "Women in Workboots" - Inspirational stories of Women who have Broken Through the Barriers in male dominated industries.

She lives in Queensland, Australia with her husband Trevor and three sons.

RECOMMENDED SUCCESS RESOURCES

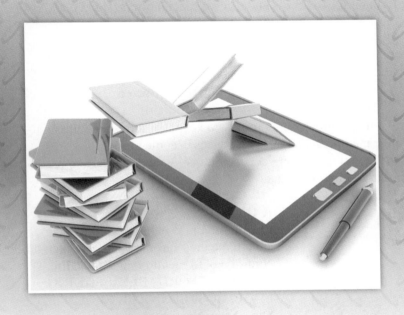

RECOMMENDED SUCCESS RESOURCES

As well as having these pages of resource information, the Women in Workboots website has more resources and can act as your main source of information. To access and receive special offers, sign up at:

www.WomenInWorkboots.com.au

There will be a greater opportunity to keep that refreshed with up to date information and as further services become available.
Make sure you like us on Facebook https://www.facebook.com/WomenInWorkboots.com.au

iCOS Live
Our mission is to help operators, to streamline their business and give them back control, not to mention time and a life. HIGHLY AFFORDABLE, LEADING EDGE, HOSTED IN THE CLOUD
http://www.icoslive.com/

Blue Steel Boots
18 Irvine Drive,
Malaga   WA   6090
08 9209 3322
http://steelblue.com.au

Eroad
Better Safer Drivers
Aust - http://www.eroad.com/au
NZ -   http://www.eroad.co.nz

Karen Scott
Kickstart Life Coaching
http://www.kickstartlifecoach.co.nz
0275 143 212

Kristie See
Executive Sales Manager Nutrimetics
0404 081 852
kristiesee@bigpond.com (Ref: WomenInWorkboots.com.au)
http://www.nutrimetics.com.au/kristiesee
Skincare, Make Up and Business Opportunities

Renovating for Profit
8 Australia Street
Camperdown NSW 2050
http://www.facebook.com.au/renoforprofit
http://www.renovatingforprofit.com.au

SALT Australia
Supporting and Linking Tradeswomen
PO Box 232 Woolongong NSW 2520
http://www.saltaustralia.com.au

Apprenticeships Melbourne
Level 2
16—20 Grimshaw Street,
Greensborough VIC 3088
http://appsmatter.com.au/

Transport Women Australia Ltd
Po Box 627
Wodonga VIC 3689
http://www.transportwomen.com.au/

Women in Mining
NSW - http://www.nswmining.com.au
QLD -http://www.womeninminingqueensland.com
WA - http://womeninmining.com/

Australian Trucking Association
http://www.truck.net.au/

Queensland Trucking Association
Transport Industry House
Suite 1, 96 Cleveland Street,
Stones Corner   Qld   4120
PH: 07 3394 4388
Email: admin@qtacom.au
http://www.qta.com.au/

South Australian Freight Council Inc.
296 St Vincent Street, Port Adelaide SA 5015
P: +61 8 8447 0635   M: +61 449 879 619
F: +61 8 447 0606
E: mccarthy.michael@safreightcouncil.com.au
W: http://www.safreightcouncil.com.au
http://www.the-linc.com.au

Take Charge of Your Money Now
http://www.StephenParrBooks.com

Pilbara Heavy Haulage Girls
http://www.pilbaraheavyhaulagegirls.com.au
https://www.facebook.com/PHHGWA

Teck-nology
For Pilbara Marketing and Business,
call today !   0427 384 285
http://teck-nology.com

Hip Pocket Toowoomba
http://www.hippocketworkwear.com.au/

**The National Association of Women in
Construction (nawic)**
PO Box 546
East Melbourne   Vict   3001
Freecall 1800 767977
http://www.nawic.com.au

Master Builders Association
http://www.masterbuilders.asn.au/
Phone: 1300 30 50 10

Branches in all Australian States
Fire & Rescue Careers
NSW - http://www.fire.nsw.gov.au
VIC - http://www.mfb.vic.gov.au/Recruitment.html
Or http://www.cfa.vic.gov.au/volunteer-careers/
career-firefighting

QLD - https://www.fire.qld.gov.au/employment/
NT - http://www.pfes.nt.gov.au/Fire-and-Rescue/
Careers-in-firefighting
WA - http://www.dfes.wa.gov.au
SA - http://www.mfs.sa.gov.au
ACT - https://esa.act.gov.au/actfr/careers
TAS - http://www.fire.tas.gov.au/
http://www.airservicesaustralia.com/careers/aviation-
rescue-fire-fighting/
http://www.defencejobs.gov.au/airforce/jobs/
FireFighter/

Fanelle
Female Apprentice Network Australia
https://www.facebook.com/SupportFanelle

Trade Up Australia
https://tradeupaustralia.com.au/

Tradie Exchange
http://www.Tradieexchange.com.au

RECOMMENDED SUCCESS RESOURCES

VET Development Centre
http://www.vetcentre.vic.edu.au

Carpentry Australia
http://www.carpentryaustralia.com.au

Auto Skills Australia
4/533 Little Lonsdale St,
Melbourne VIC 3000
(03) 8610 2500
http://www.autoskillsaustralia.com.au/